Dear You

We don't know one another, but I am going to tell you something I have told hardly anyone. Not even my own parents know. Nor do the people who were closest to me for years such as my husband and boyfriends. This is how private this secret was for me.

But things have changed over the years. I have changed. I now know that the thing I was hiding was a problem and not just some weird part of my personality. It is a problem many people suffer from and it can be pretty serious and may require professional help. I have suffered from it since I was sixteen, but today after all these years I am ready to come out of the closet and tell you:

I have an eating disorder.

Unless you have suffered from an addiction you may not realize how difficult it was just to write this down. It's quite huge, I tell you. But it also feels immensely liberating. By saying it out loud I am finally coming to terms with it and lovingly accepting this problem to be part of me. So let me say it one more time:

I have an eating disorder.

There I've said it! And now it's out. Wow! I am proud of myself! Yay!

Now my dear friend, let me tell you why I wanted to start this book by telling you this. I did it because I know I am not the only one who has suffered from an eating disorder. And my talking about this openly could perhaps help many of you out there who have a similar problem. But more important, I know I have an eating disorder, and the way I overcame it has important lessons for all of us. Most of us have an unhealthy relationship with food and our bodies. We are never satisfied with the way we look, we feel guilty when we have indulged and we label foods as being 'good' or 'bad'. That's why you're reading this book, isn't it? To get the secret mantra to looking amazing because you are not completely happy with yourself. The other day a friend of mine, laughing about being neurotic about her body said, 'You know, we all suffer from eating disorders.' She's right in a way.

I am not so different from you. I may be a well-known model and appear on TV and in films but I am also insecure, I also feel imperfect and I also have issues in life. Just like you, I don't like some parts of my body. Just like you, I have looked in the mirror and thought I wasn't thin enough. And just like you, I have read up on and tried countless diets to try and look as perfect as I want to be in my head. My eating disorder came from the pressure to always look amazing in front of the camera and from my fears that I didn't look thin enough. And now that I have finally come out of it, I can see that while it is important to look good and be fit, it is as important to learn to love yourself. And this is where you should be too, how you should feel about yourself.

You can never feel attractive and sexy unless you accept yourself and your body. I may have always been model-thin but it was never enough for me. I worried constantly about gaining weight and that fear dominated my life. So you can

PENGUIN BOOKS
HOW TO LOVE YOUR BODY

Yaana Gupta is a model, actress and singer. She was one of India's top models, the face of Lakmé and a Kingfisher calendar girl. Most recently she was a finalist on the TV show *Jhalak Dikhla Jaa*. She is currently recording her first album.

How to
Love
your
Body
and get the
body you love

YAANA GUPTA

PENGUIN BOOKS

PENGUIN BOOKS
Published by the Penguin Group
Penguin Books India Pvt. Ltd, 11 Community Centre, Panchsheel Park,
New Delhi 110 017, India
Penguin Group (USA) Inc., 375 Hudson Street, New York, New York 10014,
USA
Penguin Group (Canada), 90 Eglinton Avenue East, Suite 700, Toronto,
Ontario, M4P 2Y3, Canada (a division of Pearson Penguin Canada Inc.)
Penguin Books Ltd, 80 Strand, London WC2R 0RL, England
Penguin Ireland, 25 St Stephen's Green, Dublin 2, Ireland (a division of
Penguin Books Ltd)
Penguin Group (Australia), 250 Camberwell Road, Camberwell, Victoria
3124, Australia (a division of Pearson Australia Group Pty Ltd)
Penguin Group (NZ), 67 Apollo Drive, Rosedale, Auckland 0632, New
Zealand (a division of Pearson New Zealand Ltd)
Penguin Group (South Africa) (Pty) Ltd, 24 Sturdee Avenue, Rosebank,
Johannesburg 2196, South Africa

Penguin Books Ltd, Registered Offices: 80 Strand, London WC2R 0RL,
England

First published by Penguin Books India 2011

While every effort has been made to verify the authenticity of the information
contained in this book, the publisher and the author are in no way liable for
the use of the information contained in this book.

ISBN 9780143101680

Typeset in Sabon MT by Eleven Arts, Delhi
Printed at Thomson Press India Ltd, New Delhi

Back cover photo credits
Assistant: Prashanth Rao
Hair: Jasmine Kashung
Styling: Asha Fernandez

To India, my eternal Love,
and all its people

Contents

have a diet book that teaches you how to lose weight, but it will never be enough if you can't look in the mirror and like yourself. This is what my eating disorder taught me. How we eat, what we eat and the way we look, all happens in our head. That's why this book is not just about ways to reshape your body but also about ways to reshape your thinking. And that's why I wanted to start by telling you all the crazy issues I had about food; reading about it must make you think about the way you look at your own eating patterns as well.

We'll then move to the next part where I give you all my hard-earned lessons about eating well and being healthy. As you will see from part one, I made a lot of mistakes and these really affected my health. In my need to stay thin, I over-exercised and under-ate and it greatly affected my immune system. I am still coming out of it, and it may take me years to be totally free of it. It will take as much time as it takes to totally reprogramme my mind. I realized that the role of food in our lives is to give us pleasure and health and that I needed to focus on these two things rather than on looking hot. Having gone through every diet in the world, I finally came to some basic principles we should follow and I talk about these in part two, which also talks about exercising effectively. But as I have said, the most important part of this book is about what happens inside your head and so in part three I look at ways you can learn to love and accept yourself. This is the most important lesson of all: stay healthy, look after your body and accept it completely. Over the years, as I am slowly overcoming my disorder, I have learned to finally love and accept myself and I hope this book will help you towards that too.

Part 1
All about Me

My childhood

I was born in Brno, the second largest city of the Czech Republic, a small country that lies amid Germany, Poland, Austria and Slovakia. Some of you may know of it as Czechoslovakia. However that's like ages ago and lots of things have changed over there since then. So if you hear someone still calling it Czechoslovakia please do the Czechs and Slovaks a favour and correct them.

Brno is a very cute place with a small and beautiful old city centre. On a sunny day, it looks very romantic and you will enjoy strolling around the streets admiring the buildings. On a grey day, however (and there are plenty), you will probably just want to quickly get inside a tram or a bus and get home. For me, this is one of the strongest memories of my childhood, waiting at a bus stop, freezing (as I was somehow never adequately dressed) and complaining about the cold!

I had a wonderful childhood, though. Well, almost wonderful. Like if I could take out the fact that my parents got divorced when I was seven years old, and my sister then became a chronic drug addict and we thought she was going to die. But despite all this, it was still quite nice. I handled it somehow. I was also good at lying to myself, so when my parents finally separated I used to just think that it was better that way. But what could I do apart from repressing my feelings? It wasn't easy to lose a dad but it was better than hearing my parents scream at each other. My sister Veronika, who was two years older, didn't have it easy either. But at least we had each other and I cherish that tremendously.

I suppose it was thanks to these stressful circumstances that I was the way I was—shy, reluctant to speak, running to hide behind mom's skirt. She says I was so shy (or maybe scared) that if she left me at the playground and went away, she would find me still standing in the very same spot when she returned an hour later. I don't remember this but I do remember how she used to tell me, 'Yaana, you will never be able to eat in public! Not even bread! Look at you!' (Yes, I used to make quite a mess eating. And that has not changed. I have this unique gift of spilling things on myself whenever I eat or drink. It must be some kind of gravitational force I possess. And the gravity gets even stronger whenever I wear a white dress; strange isn't it?) But I was a cute little thing, a short, plump baby girl, with round cheeks who never threw any tantrums. So as long as you gave me my doll and fed me, I would quietly play the whole day in some corner.

Once I grew a little older I joined the primary school close to home and another life started. Studying never really interested me but what did interest me were boys. Well, not 'boys' really but a boy. Always one at a time, as of course I would never want to distribute my love. I considered love to be my life's purpose. 'What is the point of living without love?' I used to say as a ten-year-old.

Then when I turned fifteen, my world changed once again and it was all thanks to my best friend Dita.

Dita and modelling

Dita was a tall, gorgeous-looking blonde, with long legs and just the perfect measurements to become the next top Czech model. I was a much shorter, cute-looking thing, who wasn't really interested in reading fashion magazines or learning the latest make-up tricks. I would instead pack my backpack and go hitchhiking across the countryside with my friends, carrying just the bare minimum—a sleeping bag, a guitar, a knife and few cans of goulash. At night, we would find a place somewhere in the wilderness, light up a fire, cook a goulash soup, play the guitar and stare mesmerized at the stars.

However, my friend Dita was the biggest influence in my life at that time. She always got straight As, was extremely popular and had an answer for everything. She was even dating an older, extremely handsome boy who was the object of adoration of the entire female population of our school. So you see, Dita deserved some serious respect and I, who was much less popular, was in awe of her and thrilled to be her best friend.

Since Dita's dream was to become a fashion model, she often talked about it and made it sound as if it was the coolest thing in the world. So I slowly started getting interested. I had no idea who Cindy Crawford or Kate Moss were at that time but I was willing to learn quickly and she was more than willing to educate me, or should we say 'initiate' me, into the world of glamour.

After school, we would go to Dita's house. Dita would put on some music and we'd practise catwalking in the living room, walking from one corner to the other, which was just about eight steps. This was so much fun, we both loved it! Dita would then show me the latest fashion magazines or we would impatiently wait for 6 p.m. to watch our favourite programme on Fashion TV. The programme featured the latest fashion trends, spotlights on designers, make-up tips and interviews with the top models. We would never miss a show.

One day Dita came up to me after our first morning class and said excitedly, 'Yaana!!! Guess what?!!! I know how we can become models!' 'What do you mean?' I asked, just as excited. 'I found a modelling course which is held at the trade centre. It starts this Thursday at five o'clock. We have to sign up!' 'Well I don't know, I'll have to ask mom,' I said, knowing my mom would have an issue with it for sure.

'My mom is okay with it.' 'Yeah, well I don't think my mom will give me money for it, you know?'

We were always on a tight budget as mom had only a part-time job cleaning houses so she could study at the same time. My mom is quite unique that way. She has been studying something or the other her whole life; in fact the last course she finished was just two years ago. My dad used to contribute some money every month but it was quite little. He got married again and had three more children so, even though he was earning well, most of his earnings went towards his second family. So we didn't really have much money for anything apart from basic expenses and I knew that getting money for the modelling course from mom was out of the question.

'I would really love to go Dita, but I don't have the money for it,' I said with disappointment.

'It's just three thousand,' said Dita. 'I'm sure you can borrow it from somewhere.'

'Hmmm . . .' I thought for a moment. 'Maybe I could ask dad or maybe I could borrow a little money here and there and put it all together.'

'Yes, yes, yes!!!' shouted Dita and we both started jumping in excitement.

Little did I know that next Thursday would be a turning point in my life.

The modelling course

'Stand in a line and let me have a look at all of you,' said our teacher Renata, a tall, stunning woman with big, curly hair and long legs. One could easily tell she was a model as she carried herself with the grace of a queen, wore a designer suit that made her look chic and sexy yet unapproachable. She had a great figure that just called for being put on the covers of fashion magazines. Renata was just thirty-five years old but for a model that is old; so she retired from modelling and started teaching instead.

We all loved Renata instantly as she was a nice person; you could tell she loved teaching and she put her whole heart into it. Fifteen of us lined up as she took a few steps back and had a long look at us. All of us were around the same age, between fifteen and eighteen, mostly females, two men. We had all paid our fees and been admitted into the one-month course, which would end with a public fashion show, with us getting grades and a certificate. A month from now I am going to be a model, I thought to myself, hardly able to believe it. The downside was that I hadn't had the guts to tell my parents. 'You didn't tell anyone?' asked Dita, surprised as she herself was used to doing everything only after getting permission.

'Well I kind of told mom about something like this happening, you know, just casually, and she said she couldn't believe some parents would actually allow their children to get into such a thing at this age, when the kids ought to concentrate on their studies. So no, I didn't tell her I was doing this!'

'And your dad?'

'My dad, what? I haven't seen him for two weeks.'

'Oh yeah right, you did say. That's sad.'

'Yeah.'

'So you mean that no one knows you are here?'

'Well . . . he knows,' I said finally with a wide smile.

'Oh he does? Wow! What did he say?' said Dita, grinning now as this was our current favourite topic, my new boyfriend. Well, my first boyfriend to be precise.

'Eh, well not much. I don't think he knows what it means to be a model really.' Getting lost in dreams of becoming the next top model, I quickly added, 'But I'm sure he will be proud of me one day.'

'Girls?!! Have you come here to chat or learn something?' interrupted Renata.

'Now we are going to start with a pose that I have called Christy. You all know of Christy Turlington, right?'

We all nodded silently. Of course! Who wouldn't know Christy!

Renata walked a few steps and then stopped in a dramatic way, stuck out her hips on the right side, waited, letting the dramatic moment register, and then turned and headed back towards us.

We all stood there staring at her in awe.

'So this is Christy. Now we will practise this for about half an hour and then I will show you Cindy and that will be all for today.'

We then stood in a line and one by one walked the ramp and attempted to do 'Christy' while the others watched, criticizing each model among themselves. And this is what we did for the whole month. Learned how to catwalk, discussed what to wear, how to behave in a casting and how to strike poses for a fashion photographer. Three weeks into the course we were all going to do our first photo shoot, called a test shoot as these pictures were to become part of our portfolio to be shown to our potential clients at the castings. In the model's world this is just called 'the book'. The book is the most important thing for a model as that is what gets you the job.

The photo shoot (my first ever) was with a local photographer based in Brno. I can't remember his name now. He was a very nice man and made all of us very comfortable. That day we were asked to bring all our best-looking clothes with us and we had a professional make-up artist do our make-up and the stylist go through our clothes, choosing what would look the best. There was little to choose from, as you can imagine. I had the wardrobe of a fifteen-year-old girl from a struggling middle-class family. What can you expect? Dita's clothes were a bit nicer though, so I borrowed one of her shirts for the shoot. I still remember it. It was white with blue stripes and had two big round holes in the sleeves which made it look almost sexy, as sexy as you can get as a shy, nervous fifteen-year-old.

The pictures turned out beautiful and Renata loved them as well. A week later the big day came—our first catwalk where we were going to be watched by an audience of one hundred as everyone had invited their family and friends. Everyone apart from me, that is. But I didn't mind. All I cared for was that 'he' was there. He came dressed in a suit with his hair tied in a tail (he had long, dark blond hair) and I thought he looked really hot. I was a bit nervous, but being photographed and Renata's admiration had boosted my confidence big time. I felt talented, especially after seeing my pictures from the photo shoot.

I felt attractive too; I was starting to feel like a woman. The credit for that goes to my boyfriend of course. He was my first (not the first I kissed but the first with whom I enjoyed it and the first with whom I made love). That, of course, changed my entire world and it certainly showed in my body language on the ramp. Modelling after losing your virginity is a different story altogether from modelling as a virgin!

Two days later we met for the last time in the hall (which will always remain a special place for me) to receive our modelling certificates. 'I am very proud of all of you,' said Renata, making her speech sound very official even though we could see she was getting a bit emotional. 'However, some of you did better than others and while you all deserve As just for your effort and dedication, I had to distinguish the best. But please remember, to those of you who have not done as well, this is just a beginning. You can work on yourself and improve and I'm sure you will. Just take it as a challenge and work even harder, okay?' We all nodded hoping that we were not the ones she was talking about. She then gave a certificate to each of us separately, saying a few more words to the person in private. 'Yaana, you did very, very well. This is your certificate. Come to see me in my office on Monday, I need to talk to you,' she said, handing me the precious piece of paper. I had got an A+! I promised I'd be there and walked away victoriously. Dita and I then went to town and celebrated (she had got an A) by having a sundae in our favourite candy shop.

Returning home later that evening, I wondered if I should tell my mom. 'Not yet,' I thought. This is just a beginning. Let me prove myself first and get a job so then she won't be able to complain. Next Monday I went to see Renata and she told me she would like me to join the agency and start working for them. And in fact, she was also going to send me to Prague to meet another agency as 'I had too much potential to be stuck in Brno'.

Two weeks later I got my first job! It was a shoot for a catalogue for the famous cosmetic company Ahava, in Brno itself (otherwise there is really not that much happening in Brno modelling-wise). That was when I finally shared my little secret with mom and dad and everyone else. I was officially a model! Seeing that I was going to earn my first money, my parents started supporting the idea of me doing this work and even spoke to my teachers at school whenever I had to miss some classes. The money I made wasn't that much really, just three thousand crowns, but that was one-fourth of my dad's monthly salary at that time, and just for a day's work! Renata sent me to Prague, as she promised, where I met the agency. They signed me up and soon I was on a flight to Milan.

Before I go any further in this story, let's go to the big thing that started just a little before I went to Milan.

My eating disorder

See, most people think that I must have always been skinny, and that maintaining my figure must be very easy. When they ask me for my secrets and my tips, I know that they feel, somewhere deep inside, that despite anything I tell them they can never actually get into the shape I am in. Don't we all watch those good-looking people on TV and think, look how skinny that girl is! Or check out that guy's abs. Some people are just lucky to have a figure like that, aren't they?

Well I agree that some of us are born lucky. They have a faster metabolism and don't put on weight as easily as others. But I am not one of them. I love food and can gain weight pretty easily. Yet I have a career in the glamour industry, which means that I have to look good every single day. Let me tell you this is hard work. I have to constantly watch myself and I need to exercise regularly. Otherwise I'd be out of a job. I was aware of this from the very beginning of my career as even Renata used to tell us that we needed to start watching what we ate so we din't gain any weight. To me it was simple maths: more food=less job.

So I started getting conscious about what I ate and how my body looked and inevitably compared myself with models on TV, from the time Dita got me into it by showing me magazines and introducing the fashion world to me. I would admire their bodies, and wish I could be skinnier even though I definitely didn't need to lose any weight then. I didn't know then that there is a big difference between being skinny and being fit. For me these were the top models of the world and, if I wanted to become one of them, I needed to look exactly as they did.

So instead of being a happy sixteen-year-old who lives a fun teenage life, worrying about boys and what to wear to a Friday night party, I started developing a fear of becoming fat. I began to monitor everything I ate (I conned myself into calling it 'being professional'). I would forbid myself from eating anything that looked sinful (even though for others that may be just a normal meal). For example if I ate a plate of pasta, I felt instantly fat. Or even just things like dumplings, which were part of every other traditional Czech meal, I was afraid to eat as I thought I could gain weight.

Soon I started considering almost all normal food fattening unless it was steamed or cooked in water. So while my friends had a normal meal for lunch after school, I ordered a salad with a low-fat dressing on the side and made sure I ate only half of it. Of course I stared at my friends' plates wishing I could eat their food instead, but whenever such a thought crossed my mind, I would just tell myself: 'Hey! You are the one who is a model here, who gets to travel and earn money while all your friends are penniless! So some sacrifice is okay for being the lucky one here, don't you think? So keep quiet and eat your salad!' By the time my friends were done eating I would still be hungry though. I was used to having my stomach half empty and in a way I liked feeling light as it made me feel skinny but the appetite was a problem. Luckily there was a solution to this problem, a way to kill the taste buds: a cigarette. Or even better, a cigarette and coffee.

Smoking at sixteen was not that abnormal really, many teenagers do it. I started having a cigarette with coffee after meals even though I didn't even like the taste in the beginning, but well, you get used to it. I never really thought it was a cool thing to do. No doubt it was stupid. But for me the cigarette was just something that I was allowed to have as it had no calories. It was something I could have when I couldn't have food. I wouldn't smoke that much, maybe two, three a day but it was like my comfort food. And it did the trick. Whenever I felt like eating something I shouldn't, I just had a smoke and the desire would vanish.

I could do without sweets really but I did crave the traditional Czech foods my friends would eat at the pub. One of my favourites was duck with dumplings and cabbage, a typical dish we ate growing up. But when I started modelling, what do you think happened to my beloved duck? It got blacklisted. As did many other foods. Any kind of fattening meat, bread, white rice, potatoes, all cheese, pizza (of course!), dumplings, fruit that was cooked, sugar (not even one teaspoon in tea), cream (oh keep on dreaming!), normal milk (low fat was allowed as long as it was just in coffee, not a full glass of course), oh yeah and pasta (any kind that is).

I don't think I need to mention that any kind of sweet was out of the question. So much so that I began to fear my own birthday because I knew I would want to eat the cake but I couldn't. The only sweet thing I was allowed was fruit (as long as it was fresh, because preserved fruit has sugar in it) and also a bit of dried fruits and honey at times. Fruit juices were also forbidden as they are too concentrated in sugars and calories.

So what did I actually eat you may ask, right? Well, I ate a lot, don't worry! A lot of vegetables, that is. Big salads with low-fat dressing, some tuna in it here and there (tuna in a can preserved in water and not oil, mind you) and egg whites, the yellow carefully taken out, or steamed vegetables and vegetable soups. I would also have brown rice or a piece of low-fat rice cracker with it or something like that. Anything that said low calorie and fat free on the cover was good so I'd often spend hours in the shop studying all the food labels. One thing is for sure, I would never ever have bread under any circumstances. Bread was the biggest evil of all (and I am obsessed with bread by the way).

The amazing thing is that while most people would totally freak out if they were given such a diet, I actually learned to enjoy eating veggies. And luckily my most favourite food since childhood is the apple. Not even the duck beats it. But of course I hated not being able to eat like normal people. I thought it was unfair and too big a sacrifice. But then again, I told myself that it was I who chose this, and I better accept it and stop complaining.

My friends and boyfriends all rather admired the way I ate—it looked healthy from the outside because it's not that I would not eat at all in front of them. I would just eat veggies and not the yummy-looking, sinful foods they would eat. They admired me for having such a strong will and saying no to temptation, yet, at the same time, none of them wanted to be in my place. And even though I looked skinny, I never looked bulimic skinny, so no one really considered me unhealthy. And at home, they just respected that I did this job and therefore had to eat the way I did, so no one would force me into eating anything particular.

I tried keeping my mind busy just so I didn't think of food. But at night I couldn't escape my longings. In my dreams I would be eating chocolate cakes, pizza with double cheese or my darling duck. Inevitably fear would overwhelm me, a fear that I was growing fat. I can't tell you what a relief it was to wake up.

A few months into modelling, the extreme of non-eating brought on the other extreme as well—overeating. After school, I would head home skipping the school canteen lunch (I thought it was too fattening), planning to cook some veggies with brown rice at home instead. But on the way, passing by a big supermarket, I would go inside and buy myself an apple or a pear. Sometimes a friend would come with me and pick up some junk food such as my favourite Prince biscuits. Of course they would share it with me and I couldn't say no. Now it wouldn't be a big deal if I just had one or two or even three biscuits. But once I started, I couldn't stop, because it felt like a unique opportunity that wouldn't happen again. Just like if you were to give a drink to an alcoholic who's been trying real hard to abstain. I just had to finish the entire packet!

I would of course feel unhappy once I had finished the whole pack. Actually no, I began feeling unhappy as I ate it, the guilt and fear growing inside me with every biscuit I ate. It was more of a need and it didn't feel positive. Looking back I think I was just angry. Angry that I couldn't be like others and eat normally, angry that if I did eat I wasn't disciplined enough.

'It's okay,' I told myself upon finishing it. 'Tomorrow I'll start my diet again and eat only fruits the whole day, no other food! It will be like a fast and I'm sure that will help me lose what I have gained. But now since I have already sinned—which meant in my head that the day was already 'spoiled'—let me have something more to enjoy myself.' And then I'd go back to the supermarket and buy a few more things like a candy bar (or two different ones as I couldn't decide which one I wanted more and didn't want to end up feeling disappointed choosing the wrong one as this was a 'unique opportunity'), some pastry or a sandwich, simply anything with bread, and maybe even a piece of pizza. I'd start eating it right away, not even waiting to get home and I'd finish it all at breakneck speed. I'd feel really stuffed afterwards and the feeling of guilt would get worse by the minute. I'd promise myself I would never do this again, and I'd go on a proper diet from tomorrow.

The next day, I'd feel bloated and puffed up, especially on my face and around the belly. To me this was the fat I had gained, but in fact (as I learned later) it was water retention as the body tries to deal with the acidity from eating all that sugar and junk by retaining water to dilute it. And as I promised myself—but probably also to punish myself—I did eat only fruits and vegetable salads the next day so I'd lose the extra half kilo. I didn't love myself for sure. And this was just the beginning of this cycle—extreme discipline (and as I was to discover later, unhealthily so), then bingeing. How long can you go on eating vegetables and fruits, tell me? How long can you keep saying no whenever someone offers you a piece of something sweet?

I had no idea then that I had an eating disorder. I didn't even know what an eating disorder was or that it was considered an actual problem. In the beginning, the 'symptoms' were not as extreme either. I'd binge only now and then (perhaps once in two weeks) and otherwise I'd stick to my extreme diet. I was naturally skinny at the time anyway so the fear of gaining weight wasn't as big initially, which meant the pressure wasn't as much. I was also very excited to be a model so the happiness kind of kept me above the water, as it was filling up my empty stomach.

Milan

I will always remember the trip to Milan as kind of the official beginning of my modelling career. I can still remember what I was wearing on the day I landed at the airport: black stretch pants that were tight around my non-existent butt, black boots with block heels, which were comfy yet gave me the few extra inches that I needed as I already had a complex about not being as tall as the other models, and a tight black shirt that said 'Babe' by Johnson & Johnson.

I stayed with two Czech girls in an apartment that was given to us by the agency. It was a small place, with two rooms, a hall and a kitchen. None of us could speak English well so we felt a little lost. The girls would call their parents every other day and complain about feeling homesick. I called mom once a week just to assure her I was okay. I wasn't homesick at all. Ever since I was a kid I had required very little emotional support, maybe because of our difficult family background. Plus my boyfriend was going to come and visit me. Imagine, he decided to travel all the way to Milan from Brno by train and hitchhiking as he didn't have enough money for the entire trip. And all that just to spend a few days with me. See? This is called love. Thank you Mic-hal for being the coolest boyfriend ever!

Trying to get a modelling job in Milan, one of the modelling capitals and biggest fashion hubs, was tough. Each morning we would be provided a sheet of paper with addresses of all the places holding castings that day. Then we'd circle all the places on the map and be off. The whole day we would be on our feet, looking for the places, and standing in a long line of models who were lucky to have reached there earlier. The competition was huge and the women were gorgeous. It's hard to feel pretty when you're standing with a hundred beautiful models in a line.

Surprisingly, my disorder didn't get worse in Milan, because I was so excited to be a model at that time that I felt very happy. It was the beginning of everything (that's how I saw my life then) and the beginning of the disorder developing too. I didn't stare at foods I couldn't have, nor did I go and buy and eat them all then. It wasn't that bad as yet. I was too happy, which made me full from inside, so I didn't need to fill myself with food.

This is how it works with any addictive behaviour. When your life is perfect and you are extremely happy and excited, the addiction is never at its worst because you have plenty of strength to resist it and be in control. It's easy to not succumb to the addictive behaviour when you have just fallen in love or some big dream has just come true. But see, your strength lasts only as long as that extreme happiness lasts, which it never does of course. That's why people who have eating issues fluctuate in their weight a lot. Their weight loss signifies momentary happiness in their life; their weight gain reflects their unhappiness.

I was getting a bit tense about all the delicious bread though. I was trying to avoid it but it was everywhere! And all the Italian pizza, oh God! There was a pizzeria right next to our apartment in Milan where they had the thinnest pizza ever, and the girls would go there for dinner every other day while I would go to the shop next door and buy low-fat yoghurt and that would be my dinner. Believe it or not, I had pizza in Italy only once, on the last day before my departure back to Brno. And I didn't really regret it that much.

I was in Milan for only a month. My trip wasn't a success and I didn't manage to land a job. It was not just the competition, it was me. I simply wasn't tall enough for the job, at least not for the fashion shows, although for photo shoots my height wouldn't matter. I began to suffer from an inferiority complex. Big time. Of course the fact that I didn't get any work in Milan was also the fault of the agency as they were too small and insignificant to be treated seriously by the casting agencies. So while models from other agencies would have six or seven castings a day, we usually had only two, max three. The agency incidentally went bankrupt that very same year and when I heard about it I wasn't surprised at all.

Tokyo

About two months after I returned from Italy, my agency called to say that a Japanese agency was very interested in me. 'Japanese? To do modelling in Japan?' I asked, surprised, as I had never imagined it as a place to which one could travel to do modelling. The money was good. What I earned in one day, my mom would end up earning in a month.

I came back home that day very excited. 'Mom! They want me to go to Japan!'

'But you have just returned from Italy Yaana, I don't think your teachers will let you go just like that. They will think you are taking the school for a birdhouse!' (Taking something for a birdhouse is an idiom in Czech which means you don't give a damn.) Three weeks later I was on the flight to Tokyo. Mom called up the school principal and cooked up some excuse: that I was very interested in learning Ikebana (the traditional Japanese flower arrangement) and therefore a short stay in Japan would be very fruitful for my future studies. (I didn't mention that I studied in a school of gardening and park architecture did I? Well now you know.)

Tokyo turned out to be just the right market for me. The Japanese would go crazy seeing my pictures, screaming *kawayee, kawayee!!!* (Cute! Well, it's more like CUUUUUTE!!!!!!!!) Let me just point out that when Japanese women think something is kawayee, they don't just say it. No. They often literally scream out the word several times (if you are really cute, then one kawayee won't do it, you know) and they also wave their hands, clap their hands excitedly and giggle, all at the same time, before quickly rushing to cover their mouths.

Soon I became the most popular model in the agency, working almost every day and getting tons of compliments from the clients who would call up the agency to book me again and again. Thanks to being so adored I also stopped feeling insecure about my height, which wasn't an issue in Japan. My time there passed quickly—I couldn't stay longer than two months as that was the maximum length of time I was allowed to miss classes—and soon I was back home.

I was glad to be back as I was slightly homesick at the end of the trip but three months later, after I caught up on the exams back at school, I was already itching to return to Tokyo. I had gotten used to being out of my parents' sight and doing whatever I liked, the way I liked it. And I was loving it. I started to feel more like an adult, being all on my own in a foreign country and it made me grow as a person much faster than my friends who were sitting back home. Earning my own money at that age was a big deal too, especially because we never had much money to begin with. Now thanks to modelling I hadn't taken even a crown from my parents since the age of sixteen.

Back in Tokyo I picked the biggest agency, which also happened to be the best there was, and went to meet them, showing them my book and the list of jobs I had done on my earlier trip. They signed me right away (generally it's not that easy, agencies are very picky about who they decide to sign up), so I dictated my own terms and we shook hands on it. The agency's apartments were in the middle of Roppongi, which was really the place to be. Most of their models were put up in the same building, which had several apartments per floor, girls sharing with girls and guys with guys. It was at this point that my eating disorder really developed.

I knew that I had to keep myself fit to do the job and the pressure got even greater when I started shooting for lingerie catalogues. You need to be in perfect shape you see, so you can't just go out and eat pizza every day or whatever it is you wish, or so I thought. I took my job seriously because it was a job, not a hobby. It was my bread and butter, so I could never act unprofessionally and sticking to my fat-free diet and working out was just a part of the job.

So when we stopped to buy lunch between castings and the girls headed to Mc Donald's, I'd go to Seven-Eleven (a chain of grocery stores) and buy an apple, yoghurt and a salad. I have to say the other girls admired me for eating this 'healthy', often commenting that they wished they could be more like me. What I actually wished for was to be more like them. But I just couldn't. I had by now become scared of food. I felt that if I had one bite, I wouldn't be able to stop myself and would end up eating not just one burger but at least two. And that was the problem. The pressure of not eating inevitably made me want to eat in excess.

See this is what happens when you try to restrain yourself from doing something you are not really ready to give up. For example, let's say you decide to be celibate for a certain amount of time, I can guarantee you that you will be thinking about sex the whole day. Similarly, all I thought about was food. My entire day revolved around the next meal I was going to eat, where I was going to get the healthy non-fat stuff, did I have enough healthy stuff on me, did I have enough veggies in the fridge, etc.

My regular diet at that time was about three apples, three carrots, two salads, two plain yoghurts and a soup at night. The yoghurts were non-fat and the soup was clear. I remember standing in the store, dithering over a corn soup that had a hundred calories and a carrot soup that had eighty-nine calories, and finally choosing the second option. In the evening I would have a huge mug of coffee, run to the gym and work out like mad. My calorie-burning target was a thousand calories even if I had to crawl my way back home. What an unhealthy lifestyle! I'm amazed I didn't collapse.

Just to remain sane, I decided that one day a week I would allow myself to eat whatever I wanted. Whenever I went to the Seven-Eleven I would check out the bread section and look at all the yummy things and then wait for Friday evening. If you were a fly on the wall, watching me pig out in front of the TV, you wouldn't be able to believe the amount of food I ate! I would generally eat a sandwich, a tub of Häagen-Dazs ice cream either with chocolate chip cookies or macadamia nuts, some cookies and some pastries. The next day I invariably felt disgusted with myself.

I had no idea I was suffering from an eating disorder back then. I thought I just lacked self-control because if I ate normal food I would always overeat. So I avoided food like a devil does the cross (as we say in Czech). Not being able to eat normally made me constantly edgy as I had to keep planning my meals and looking for low-fat options or carry the food with me and that was just a headache.

I can tell you whenever I ate out I used be every waiter's nightmare. I would always ask for things that were not on the menu, pretty much creating my own meal. Sometimes I would insist on the chef coming to take my order. Other times, I would make the waiter write it down so he could remember everything. I would ask for there to be no cream, no cheese, no milk, no mayonnaise or other dressing or sauce, no bread or bread croutons, no egg yolk, no oil, no butter, no flour, no corn, no olives, and of course no sugar or syrup. And this was just part of the list! In spite of this I sometimes found the meal I was served too greasy, and I would mop it up with my friend's bread. I can't believe I lived like this for seventeen years. Of course I was used to it, so only now do I see how crazy it was. My life wasn't normal. I couldn't even go on a vacation and enjoy the local food and feel easy about it.

I have to say though that I didn't look unhealthy skinny, just plain skinny, so no one ever suspected I had any kind of eating disorder. The only eating disorders that are really noticeable are anorexia and bulimia because the person ends up looking stick thin. But let's get back to the poor insecure teenage me who was just trying to become this perfect version of herself, the skinniest version that is. I remember a picture of me taken in my apartment in Tokyo. It was one of my favourite pictures of myself as it showed my cheekbones, which were otherwise pretty invisible. I always had an obsession with prominent cheekbones as my favourite models (Eva Herzigova and Christy Turlington) had them and it seemed to be the 'in' thing. (Oh God this is making me laugh real hard right now!) I also wanted to have this vertical line going through the middle of my stomach, you know what I mean, right? The perfect belly basically! At that time it didn't occur to me that I couldn't have both these things because my body structure simply isn't like that! But I believed that till I got my belly to look like that I wouldn't be 'perfect'. Can you imagine, it took me like fifteen years to finally give up on that belly.

Goodbye Tokyo

The first few years in Tokyo were fun. I partied a lot—in fact looking back at that time, I still can't imagine how I could have done all the partying I did! I also loved the attention, earning good money, meeting people from all corners of the world and travelling wherever I wanted to. But after three years the work became monotonous. How long can you go on making money just by looking pretty? How long will you enjoy sitting in front of a mirror for a few hours every day (while your make-up is being done), and then changing from one outfit to another and striking poses for the camera? Sooner or later it becomes boring just as any other job where you're doing the same thing every day and not learning anything new.

So while I had loads of work in Japan and earned well, I was not happy. I couldn't find any meaning in the work I was doing. It all seemed so shallow and repetitive. I felt so alone—alone in Tokyo, one of the most populated cities in the world. It had partly to do with me feeling restless. I couldn't relate to anyone, couldn't have a meaningful discussion with anyone. But it was also their culture. You can live in Japan for years but as long as you are a foreigner, you will always be looked at as one. In fact many people from the older generation who had lived through World War II would often give you a nasty look while passing you in the street, as if you were responsible for dropping the nuclear bomb upon them. So one day I just packed my bags and left. It wasn't Japan that I was trying to escape, it was modelling, and well, I suppose, me as well. I had a list of places I could have gone to but there was a place that I had always been attracted to. India.

When I was sixteen years old, just about the time I was starting my modelling career, I and my best friend Veronika decided to spend our New Year's holiday in a meditation centre in a village 20 kilometres away from Brno. We had no clue what to expect there but we were intrigued by the word meditation and the whole spiritual business. I was reading *The Tibetan Book of the Dead* at the time so when my mom (who had visited the centre for a yoga weekend earlier that year) mentioned this centre to us we both got curious. That week I was introduced to a whole new world, a world of meditation and spiritual seeking. The people I met in the centre were also part of a new world, a world that seemed so much more real than the one I was used to living in. And so I felt, as I came to the end of the road in Japan, that perhaps I would find a new path in India.

Hello India

I turned twenty-one the day I set foot in India. Little did I know that this day was the beginning of my new life. All I knew was that I didn't want to live the life I had left behind. I was done with modelling and with my past. I didn't know how I would earn money but I didn't give a damn as I had a little bit of money saved and in India I could make it go a long way.

After a short stay in Goa (you know it's mandatory for all visitors to India) I took an overnight bus to Pune where I rented a room in Koregaon Park and started visiting the Osho ashram. Every morning I would get up at 5.30 a.m., walk ten minutes to the ashram and join the first meditation of the day, which starts at 6 am. I would attend various meditation sessions through the day taking just few breaks in between, walking inside the ashram area or sitting somewhere reading a book. I would leave for home only at night when the last meditation was over. Soon I started feeling much more at peace with myself and decided to extend my stay in India.

Another reason for not wanting to leave was a man I met at the ashram a few weeks after my arrival. His name was Satyakam, and he had been living in Pune for fourteen years. We immediately connected though he was fourteen years older than me. I remember the day he walked up to me saying he had seen me at the ashram and he wanted to give me one of his paintings. It sounds quite romantic, doesn't it? Well Satyakam was a special kind of guy and pretty innovative I have to say. He was way too smart to try any of the regular pick-up lines, or maybe he knew I wasn't the kind who'd be easily bullied into a date as I really came to the ashram to meditate and not pick up men. So you know what he did after presenting me with the painting? Nothing! I mean like totally nothing. He just gave it to me, said goodbye and went to the ashram kitchen to continue his work. (He wasn't a cook by the way, it's just one of the things you can do at the ashram—it's called a working meditation.)

I was of course stunned that this man didn't even try to hit on me any further as that's what I had imagined he would do (he really is a smart guy, you know). But as I said he was quite mature and experienced so he knew how to go about it.

And this is a lesson for all of you gentlemen. If you want to get the woman of your dreams all you have to do is to leave your bait hanging there and then pretend you are not at all interested and the woman comes to you by herself. And that is what happened.

A few days later, I decided to perform at an open-mic night and, as I needed a guitarist to accompany me, and I knew Satyakam played the guitar, I went to the kitchen to find him. Within a week we had decided to get married. Yes, that's true; I am not exaggerating. That is how quick it was. And even though today we are not together (we separated five years later) I will always say that I made the right decision by marrying him.

My life in Pune

We got married three months later as we needed to register at the court before we could get a date for the wedding. On the big day I wore the best clothes I had (a black shirt and jeans) while Satyakam wore his best kurta and then we headed to Pune's marriage court on a scooter accompanied by two of Satyakam's friends—our witnesses (whom I never saw afterwards by the way). Satyakam was quite a loner like me so when we realized we needed someone to witness our marriage he had to think real hard to find someone to do it for us. After the wedding we went to Prem's, one of our favourite Koregaon Park restaurants, and had lunch with our two witnesses. There is just one photo that documents our marriage and that was the photo taken at the restaurant. Now you may find this to be quite a sad marriage celebration but to both of us it didn't matter. This is what happens when you marry someone for love. You don't really care about the trappings of a marriage ceremony—as long as your loved one is there, that's all you need.

Soon after that I shifted my suitcase to Satyakam's apartment consisting of one small room, a toilet and a tiny kitchen and we were set for our life together. The rent for the place was just 1500 rupees (the rate very much reflected the state of the apartment) so we didn't have to worry about our income for a while. Satyakam wasn't really earning as his focus was on meditating, but now and then he would make a painting and sell it for a few thousand rupees and that would take care of his expenses—he did lead a frugal life. I too had some money in the bank in Japan so we managed to survive on that for a long time.

Our life together was simple and relaxed, filled with love and inspiring conversations that generally revolved around life and spiritual experiences. Every morning we would go to the ashram, each of us doing our own thing and we'd meet again back at home in the afternoon when Satyakam would start painting and I would try to learn things from him, play the guitar or attempt to make jewellery pieces from silver and beads.

I also joined a local gym to keep myself fit but the sense of being on a permanent holiday with no modelling work around the corner allowed me to take it quite easy. It was the first time since the age of sixteen that I could stop thinking about the way I looked, not wear any make-up or spend time on deciding what to wear every day. In the ashram everyone wore a maroon robe so all I had to do was pick between robe number one or two.

My life was so simple then. I also began to finally eat just like everyone else and stopped studying my belly in the mirror afterwards, which was a totally liberating experience. I didn't have to worry about the food being too oily or containing too many calories, knowing I didn't have to wear a bikini the next day. I felt like my soul had finally got a chance to recover from its hurtful past of food madness. My favourite food was dosa with coconut chutney or the Hyderabadi biryani that we ate at a cheap restaurant near our home. I didn't miss modelling at all, nor did I miss Tokyo or my past lifestyle. I thought that perhaps I might have to return when my savings ran out but the thought wasn't appealing. I was learning to make jewellery and I had even signed up for a computer course so I had a vague hope that something might come out of these one day.

A year of this blissful existence passed by quickly and soon I had to wake up to the fact that my bank balance was getting low. It was time to start looking for work again. Knowing I wasn't keen on returning to Japan, Satyakam suggested that perhaps I should try to get some modelling assignments in Mumbai. I bought all the Indian fashion magazines and looked at the editorial sections to check which were shot locally and noted down the names of the photographers. I would then google those names, get their official websites, find their contact information and write an email to each photographer. Luckily for me, I came across the best photographers in the country including Farrokh Chotia, Daboo Ratnani, Vikram Seth and others. In fact Farrokh told me recently that he has saved that email of mine—and now it's been ten years! Daboo was the first to reply, saying he had something for me if I was interested. It was a shoot for a designer, Arjun Khanna, and even though I wouldn't be paid I'd get the pictures from the shoot. I agreed of course. I didn't need pictures, but I realized this could be the beginning of a work relationship.

A week later I went to Mumbai and did my first shoot in Mumbai! If I remember right, this was in March 2001. By April I had signed a contract with Lakmé, the biggest cosmetic brand in India. Being the Lakmé girl was a dream come true for any model in India. I had no clue how big it was initially but I slowly understood its significance when I started getting calls from journalists wanting to interview me just a week after I had signed the contract.

Everything was going unbelievably well. My husband and I shifted to a one-bedroom apartment in Bandra. I was soon everywhere, in posters, magazines, on TV. In a matter of three months I had already worked with the biggest photographers and done fashion shows for the biggest designers. It was like a dream come true. I was so thrilled to be able to walk on the ramp as that's what I had always wanted to do but had never managed to because of my height. In India however, although I was one of the smallest girls on the ramp, no one seemed to care. You may be wondering how come I didn't mind modelling again when I was so against it, right? Well a year's break and a normal life and meditation helped a lot, but it was mainly the industry and the people that were different. Of course the glamour industry is pretty superficial wherever you go, but in India I felt people were just nicer human beings so that made a big difference to me.

Everything was amazing apart from one thing: my body. While everyone seemed to like me (and my body) just fine, I didn't. The biryani didn't just 'evaporate' you know. I must have put on two or three kilos at least over the year in Pune, but I felt as if I had gained five and I was extremely uncomfortable with it. Luckily as no one knew how skinny I was before, no one gave me those 'oh you have put on so much weight' comments. But I knew and I thought about it day and night.

My old fears resurfaced. I felt fat again. So I went through a few bookshops and bought all the diet books I could find.

However no miracle diet book was as promising as its title and they all just added more foods to the list of what not to eat. So by the time I was done reading, I figured there wasn't much I could put on my plate. This wasn't really encouraging but I was willing to do anything to get back in shape fast. So I ate fat-free, sin-free meals and at the same time did tons of cardio in the gym every day. My typical diet would be sugar-free muesli for breakfast with plain yoghurt, salad for lunch and some steamed or baked fish with vegetables for dinner. One of my favourite salad recipes that I developed at that time was tomatoes with grated beetroot and one spoon of soy mayonnaise. It was yummy! So I didn't feel bad about not eating the other delicious Indian foods but I do have to say that when my husband ordered a burger, I often escaped to the bedroom to read a book just so I wasn't tempted looking at him.

At work however, I wasn't left with much option as all the models would eat a buffet meal at the five star hotels where we did the ramp shows. So I generally ended up having yellow dal and rice as I believed it to be the least fattening. I also made sure I got up early in the morning and did an hour in the gym in the hotel we were put up in even if we were all taking a morning flight and hadn't gotten much sleep. I was the only female model who was so anal about gymming though. Sometimes I would bump into a few male models in the gym who were much more conscious about their body, but out of the females I remember seeing only Sheetal Mallar walking on a treadmill in the gym and that too just once.

The models were all quite skinny. Perhaps not as skinny as the ones abroad, and a few even had curves, but most of them were just the usual bones, no-ass, no-boobs type. Most of them didn't really care about whether the food they ate was fattening or healthy, and it remains a mystery to me how they stayed that skinny. I suppose they all ate very little (I never saw any model eating a plate full of food) and some may have perhaps been bulimic, you never know. It's not something the girls talk about amongst themselves you know? In the world's top fashion cities, where the competition is tough and the demands are more strict, you'd get to see some very skinny women whom you knew instantly were bulimic or heavily into drugs. In India, some of the models smoke dope before going on the ramp, which I suppose burns off quite a few calories or shifts the interest from food to the drugs and the party afterwards, but at the time that I was in the industry in India, I didn't feel that drugs were all over the place (maybe because I always stayed away from them).

Eventually I did lose some weight, but the thing was I couldn't lose all of it and at some point the weight loss hit a plateau so that last bit of fat on my belly just wouldn't go away! I was painfully conscious of it and every time a fashion show came up, I would pray not to get any outfits that revealed my stomach, such as a choli and ghagra. But of course I did get plenty of those and there was nothing I could do apart from hoping that the designer would wrap the duppata in such a way that it covered my tummy.

This belly of mine was always my weak spot as I have told you. I just couldn't accept it the way it was. To me it was ugly. In fact even while making love I would get so conscious when my beloved touched my stomach that I immediately sucked it in, in a snail-like reflex. And I was so uneasy about my belly that if a guy brought his hand anywhere close to it, I would just catch hold of his hand and guide it elsewhere. I was also not very comfortable being seen naked. Even when I walked past my husband, I would either try to cover my stomach with something or stand straight, pull it in and quickly cross him hoping not to be noticed very much.

I wondered how other women did it. Was I the only one who acted this weird? I could understand behaving like this the first time you were with someone, but acting like this in the presence of someone you had been with for years? That's weird no? I always reasoned I was this insecure only because I was comparing myself to other models. But then I realized that it was just in my head because I was not dating male models, but normal men and none of them had dated a model before and surely I'd be a dream come true for them! That would make me relax and laugh at myself a little, but not completely. Once you are insecure in your head, you find plenty of excuses. Even if there are people telling you how beautiful you are every single day, all you will think is, 'Oh what do they know!'

Diets!

As my career thrived, my eating disorder was much more in control, that is I binged less. I was inspired by the work and I suppose doing so well for myself also made me feel quite high and positive. However during this period I got on to a whole load of diets. I have tried every one in the book. One day my husband brought home a book on a diet I'd never heard of before and following it made a huge difference to my weight loss. It was the low carbohydrate diet by Atkins, one of the most dangerous diets ever. I didn't know that of course so I happily cut down on all the rice and dal and stopped eating any carbs whatsoever (apart from a few fruits here and there but even that I limited). I loved this diet! Upon entering hotel rooms, I would open the minibar and eat a can of cashews and enjoy it without any fear. For breakfast I would eat cheese with some veggies (no bread though) and have a coffee with full-fat cream. My weight dropped noticeably and for the first time my belly almost disappeared.

By the third month, however, the weight loss stopped together. But what was worse, I started feeling very weak. I then started depending on coffee just to get through the day or else I would feel exhausted, listless and drowsy. Each morning I started by having two espresso shots just so I could get myself to the gym and work out. By lunch I was already dead again so I'd have another one. And as I worked out twice a day at that time—so obsessive was I—I would have to have another two shots just before I headed to the gym the second time.

Four months on, I had zero energy and was left with only crazy cravings for sugar. My workout routine was also killing me. It all came to a head one evening. I was waiting to have dinner with a friend at a Chinese restaurant in Taj Lands End in Bandra when I suddenly started feeling so weak (I had just completed an hour-long run on a treadmill at the Taj gym) that I excused myself to go out for some fresh air. I was terrified of fainting in public and quickly headed to the swimming pool area. My friend who had come out with me held me, feeding me sachets of white sugar, one after another. With this my low-carb dieting came to an official end.

The biggest victim of all this was my health. From the outside, I looked perfectly healthy and even strong. I could run for an hour on a treadmill, faster than anyone else, or sprint up a flight of stairs leaving others far behind me. But my immunity was always very low. I was falling sick every forty days and it was always the same cycle. First I would get a cold, the next day a fever, and two days later I'd be coughing my lungs out. This would go on for two weeks. The cycle would then repeat every forty days even though I tried hard to be good and ate lots of fruits and supplements, went to the sauna twice a week and visited all kinds of therapists. I tried allopathic medicine, antibiotics, homeopathy, Ayuverda, but none of it helped. It was as if someone had laid a curse on me. Today I know it was me and only me who was responsible for my ill health. I had made myself this weak by eating what diet books prescribed and not what my own body actually needed.

Meeting Cuckoo

One man changed it all. While on holiday in Goa, I met a friend who told me he was cured by a Taiwanese acupuncture doctor in Goa. It got me all curious about this man they called Cuckoo as he was supposedly a Zen master. So the next morning I took a taxi to Candolim beach where I found his clinic, among the local Goan houses.

The place was filled with patients waiting for the magic doctor to arrive so I sat there and waited too. At 10 a.m. a small man dressed in a white, Chinese-looking kurta appeared at the clinic. He had long, black hair and a long, thin beard and must have been in his fifties. But he was so sprightly and eneregtic that I thought he was younger. I didn't take my eyes off him as he sat on a chair, listening to each patient carefully. Every now and then he'd jump to his feet and rush into one of the mosquito-net-like tents where he would quickly stick a few needles into a patient.

When my turn came I sat next to him ready to tell him about my health issues but he quickly caught my wrist and signalled for me to remain still. He then froze and stared into the distance as if he was about to read my destiny. I was afraid to even breathe.

'Your lungs!' he suddenly screamed out excited. 'You problem to breath, yes?' he said not waiting for any confirmation.

I nodded silently.

'You have man? You in re-ation-ship?' he asked in his heavy accent.

'You not so happy, yes?'

I didn't know what to say. My marriage with Satyakam was unravelling and we would separate shortly and divorce a year later in 2006. This man knew way too much!

'Come, I give you needle and medicine and you feel better,' he got up leading me under the mosquito net.

I lay down ready to surrender my life into this man's hands.

'But this problem in your mind!' he said with a huge grin pointing at his head while I was trying to focus on his eyes and not look at the needles he was now sticking into my legs, arms and head. I had no time to react to those words as I was now covered with needles.

Each time a needle penetrated my skin, it would sting a little and an electric sensation would course through my entire body. A few seconds later any signs of pain or discomfort would disappear, unless I tried moving of course. So I was literally pinned down to the bed and was rescued only forty five minutes later when one of Cuckoo's students came and took the needles out.

I stood up slowly, expecting pain to shoot up my legs, but nothing happened so I carefully made my way out of the mosquito tent and headed to the nearby table to pick up my medicine. Cuckoo was on the other side of the room busy attending to other patients so I thought I'd say a quick goodbye, pay and leave. But when I approached him he smiled at me as if we'd known each other for years, held my arm and said, 'You eat some Taiwanese food? You go bitch and come here twelve?'

Why is he calling me a bitch? I wondered.

'Oooh . . . you mean a beach? I go to the beach and come back at twelve?' I finally understood.

'Yes! You go bitch and come back and we eat, okay? Taiwanese food very good for you!'

'Okay, I come back,' I happily agreed, feeling special as he was not offering this to every one of his patients.

An hour later I headed back to Cuckoo's home, which was by the clinic. There were five people sitting around chatting, all Cuckoo's students (or disciples if you want). Cuckoo came out of the kitchen, handed me an empty plate and led me inside to a table laden with food. Some baked fish, pork, miso soup, rice, a funny looking vegetable and a salad. He reached out for the pork to serve me but I refused.

'Ooooh, you are vegetable?' he asked.

'Yes I am a vegetarian,' I replied smiling at his English.

'Your blood type. What's your blood type?'

'I'm B plus, I think,'

'Ooooooh, now I know! This not good for you! You need fish! All B type need fish. That's why you weak!'

'But I don't like to eat meat,' I objected.

'Oooh, this in your head. You try one month and you see! If your health no good, then you don't eat, okay?'

'Okay Cuckoo, I try,' I said and I meant it.

I would have tried anything then as I was tired of being sick again and again. And yes, perhaps it wasn't good for me to be vegetarian as I had after all stopped eating meat only after coming to India. We all sat down to eat our lunch while Cuckoo led the conversation in his 'smash' English as he called it. Everyone around the table seemed to understand his heavy accent, while I really had to pay attention to every word he was saying.

Cuckoo talked about some of his patients or friends back in Taiwan, always interspersing it with a few jokes or showing us some of the acupuncture points. He even said he would teach me a few points if I wanted so I could help cure my cough whenever I got one. I happily agreed and so he stuck a needle in one of my hands and said, 'Now you try! Here!' he said pointing at the same spot on my other hand.

I took a needle and guided by his hand I pierced it in a point called 'hoku' which was supposed to be the universal point that every acupuncturist would have to pierce in every session as it releases over-all tension in the entire body.

'Ooooh, you good student! No fear!' he said watching me inserting the needle deeper.

'You don't scare anything huh?' he added and I was proud of myself I have to say.

'You come tomorrow and I teach you more, okay?'

'Okay!' I said excited as ever.

And thus I officially became a student of Cuckoo.

Cuckoo has truly changed my life like no one else ever did or ever will I suppose. He is my master. He teaches me not just acupuncture but he teaches me about life as well. It took only a couple of months for me to stop falling ill altogether. I have never had bronchitis since, which to me is a miracle as I suffered from bronchitis since I was seven. I stopped being a vegetarian too and today I eat not only fish but also lamb on occasion.

What Cuckoo taught me

Cuckoo believes that all answers are hidden within us and all we need to do is pay attention and listen to our own body. 'The experience is what matters, not the knowledge' is what Cuckoo says and thanks to listening to him, not only has my health improved tremendously but my understanding about food, diet and my body has moved in quite a different direction.

Before I met Cuckoo, I was used to trusting whatever I read in books, and never thought that I should listen to my body and try to follow its signals to figure out if the things I was reading about and applying were actually good for my body—and at times also for my soul (and my mind). I would be very rigid with my diet and my exercise routine, as what I believed in my head was the ultimate and my body just had to follow it, because it was surely the best, right? This attitude is what made me hurt my body.

Each one of us has certain qualities and behaviour traits we need to be aware of. According to Ayurveda, there are three main types of people: *vata*, *pitta* and *kapha*. All three types have distinctive qualities and knowing which type you are helps you understand yourself on various levels. For me, it was very helpful when I learned that I am a vata type as it made me understand why I behave the way I do (impulsively for example) and why some of the things I was eating were making me feel out of balance. We also all have our own body types. It's important to understand what body type you have so you know what food is the best for you, and what food you should avoid to keep healthy and fit. And we all have slightly different requirements because of this. Remember when Cuckoo said I should be eating more fish and meat?

Getting to know yourself really helps your head. It's like having a roommate that you get to know little by little each day and the more you know this roommate, the less you mind if she leaves dirty dishes in the sink or keeps her underwear hanging in the common bathroom (so your boyfriend has to make his way through it, if he wants to wash his hands). You can learn how to accept her and even learn to love her for the way she is.

So the more you get to know yourself, the more you will know how to make yourself happy, you see. Because it's you and you alone who can make yourself happy. So you need to spend lots of time studying yourself, literally, being aware of how you react in certain situations or why you think the things you think or feel the things you feel. It's all one never-ending self study.

And the more awareness you bring into it, and the more often you focus on learning and understanding yourself, the better. It's just like cooking a Thai curry. If you cook a Thai curry once a month, you have to follow the recipe each time you do it, because you don't remember how to make it. But if you start cooking the Thai curry once every few days, soon the curry starts tasting real different, quite special I'd say. And everyone who tastes it will love it for sure. And that's how you will know that you really learned it well.

As they say, for others to love you, you first need to learn how to love yourself. Hence:

Learn how to cook real well.

Cuckoo's teachings are very subtle. He doesn't sit down and tell you okay, pull out your notebook and write this down. I learn the most by watching how he lives and behaves with his own body. For example if we were celebrating the Chinese New Year and drank quite a bit at night, the next morning you'd see him puncturing himself with needles, drinking two litres of water with tonnes of active calcium in it (calcium neutralizes the acid in the body) or see him prepare special Chinese teas or a soup made of seaweed. If we went for a dinner outside and had a meal that wasn't the healthiest, he'd say: 'This is nooo ploblem! You just enjoy! Later we have shitting tea, okay?'

He is always aware of the energy in his body, knowing when exactly he needs to rest and take it easy or when he can be active the whole day, go to his farm, go fishing, travel to visit his patients, stay up late talking to us or take it easy and retire early or take a nap during the day. He often says, 'Respect your body!' and you see how he practices what he teaches.

I learn the most from him when I go to him with a specific issue. Once, for example, I was in Peru and got bitten by mosquitoes in the Amazon jungle so badly that my face swelled up and the swelling wasn't going away as I apparently had an allergic reaction to it. I was getting tense because in a few days I was supposed to shoot an ad for Lakmé in India. Luckily my return flight from Peru was via Amsterdam and Cuckoo happened to be there at that point. So I stopped over for a few days, and he gave me needles, cupping, and made a special liver-cleansing tea for me three times a day that was made of some Chinese pickled root vegetable and tasted salty and nice. After just a day I could see the swelling going down and by the time I faced the cameras in Mumbai my face looked as if nothing had ever happened to it.

Cuckoo treats me in such a fatherly way. We may be sitting at a dinner with some people; he will be talking when suddenly he hears me cough. He pulls out a needle, sticks it in my neck and continues talking as if nothing has happened. Then he will wink at me and say, 'cough finish, no?' I don't even have to reply. Of course it's gone and he knows it.

Once I was shooting a TV commercial for a hair spray where I had to run in high heels in a parking lot as I was being chased by kidnappers. I fell and twisted my ankle so badly that I was taken to a hospital right away. Torn ligament was the diagnosis. I refused painkillers and called up Cuckoo. 'You know this!' he said. 'I teach you this point before! It's on your left hand, remember? One and half inch long needle!' 'Oh yes! I remember!' I took out the needles I carry in my purse and stuck the correct one in my hand. 'Ouch! I hate this one Cuckoo!' I complained. He laughed. 'You see! Your leg okay in no time!' And he was right. The doctors told me it would take at least a month to heal. I was walking in two weeks with no issues, and I felt no pain at any point and didn't need the painkillers.

Cuckoo's healing is true magic. And it's wonderful to see that you don't even need to use allopathic medicine at most times. The only time I allowed allopathic medicine to enter my body was when I had surgery on my nose after I broke it dancing in *Jhalak Dikhla Jaa*. And if Cuckoo had been there with me, I wouldn't have needed it as he could have given me a needle that works as an anaesthetic.

Cuckoo's main emphasis is on the mind though. He believes (and it is what his thirty years of experience have taught him) that most human disease is caused by the mind, because it is our mind that creates thoughts that bring us emotions that can create blocks in the paths of energy through our bodies when they are not dealt with, released or faced. You often hear him say personal things to clients after he checks their pulse, making a diagnosis. 'You get angry quick, yes?' he'll say or: 'You very emotional, yes? You pain in your heart? Not good for you too serious! Life is just a game! Come on! You just enjoy! Don't think too much, okay?'

This is what I love about Cuckoo. He is not the master who sits in white clothes in front of you and talks in a slow meditative voice (giving a satsang). He screams out passionately when he speaks, he jokes and uses words like shit and fuck and makes everyone laugh. He'll even stand on a table and dance. He'll never miss a chance to have fun. And I love that about him. He doesn't try to live some 'godly' life, giving up worldly pleasures as if they were something bad, something unspiritual, something we should give up in order to be 'good' or become enlightened. He is a true human and not someone who projects that he is different from (and superior to) others because he has understood life. In fact, to that he'd say, 'It's all bullshit. You need to learn how to take care of your life and your body. No need to sit and do meditation. Daily life is the real meditation!'

With his own life Cuckoo shows his students that it's important to learn how to live in the real world surrounded by the city, money, fame, stupidity, mistakes, problems and the simplest things. What's the point of knowing how to be at peace when one is sitting in a lotus position in the Himalayas? Can you be at peace when you are in the middle of Mumbai's traffic and honking? Can you? Real life is here and the spiritual lessons hide in everyday life's situations. And so to me, Cuckoo represents life. REAL life. And that's why I take him as my master.

It's after meeting Cuckoo that I slowly began to come to an awareness of my attitudes towards food and my body. I realized how full of fear I was and how insecure. It wasn't an instant journey. It would take four years for me to finally break out of the cycle. But it all began in Goa that day.

How I finally tackled the eating disorder

Cut to the summer of 2009. For the first time, after fifteen years, I had decided to live in Brno again. Being back after so long, I felt a strong desire for the typical Czech cuisine. Now, however, I could allow myself to relax as I was not doing any modelling nor was I going back to India to do any other work as I wanted to focus on my music. With Cuckoo in my life, my eating had improved a lot. Around the same time I met him, I had also came across a book by Bill Phillips, an international fitness trainer who was famous for getting people in shape. The book said the exact opposite of what I had learned in all the diet books I had ever read (you see, diet books and fitness books often have nothing in common). The message was that in order to lose weight and get fit you need to eat.

Now this was a revelation for me! And this is when I finally, after years of starving, started to eat. My daily diet would consist of five small meals a day (sometimes even six if I got up early) always combining a portion of carbs with portions of protein and some vegetables. I shall give you the exact details of this diet in the diet section of the book as that is what I eat today. I also began to weight train in the gym instead of just doing crazy cardio. Allowing myself to eat properly and not restricting my gym routine to cardio helped me get into the best shape I have ever been in my life. Training with weights also made a huge difference. I started building muscle (finally got a proper butt) and lost that last bit of weight.

But although I was eating much more healthily, had my thinking really changed? The point wasn't just about getting the perfect eating formula, it was also to stop feeling anxiety or guilt if I wasn't eating healthy all the time (and this is my message in this book). I was in a pub that summer having lunch with my sister. After going through the menu, I settled on some baked fish and veggies but what I really wanted to have was the duck and dumplings I used to love as a child.

When the food was finally laid on our table, I looked at my boring dish and confessed to my sister about having this fear of food for years.

'I think I must be crazy! I am just obsessed with food! I think of it all the time!' I told her. 'I don't think anyone can possibly think of food as much as I do! And I'm really tired of it now, you know. I just want to eat normally and not think about it for God's sake! It's driving me crazy!'

'I'm surprised to hear you say that,' said Veronika. 'I always envied you for being fit. I thought you were just okay eating the stuff you do!'

'No I am far from okay! I don't think this is normal. I may have a very strong will and stick to these crazy diets, but deep inside I am really disturbed by not being able to relax about food just like everyone else. Food should just be food, something you enjoy but you don't live for. It shouldn't be taking so much space in your mind, should it?'

'Well I totally know what you're saying Yaana. I have the same problem. I think of food all the time. I'm unhappy with the way I look so I try to diet all the time but at times I just can't take it and I have to binge like crazy! That makes me gain weight of course which makes me feel unhappy so I go back to dieting. It's a vicious cycle.'

'You do? Me too!' I said shocked to hear this coming from her.

'You too? No way! Really?' she was just as surprised.

We spent hours that night telling each other what we had gone through over the years. Later that night I thought of our conversation and decided to look for some books on the topic as I was now persuaded this must be a mental problem, not just a lack of will. I went on the net and searched Amazon for books on eating disorders, found a few that had the word bingeing in the title and ordered them. The books turned out to be very helpful. It was an eye-opener reading cases of other people having the same issue and identifying with it. It made me feel more normal and not alone. It also made lots of sense. One of the first things the books suggested was that I should make a promise to myself never to go on any diet under any circumstances. Then I was supposed to buy all the foods I ever liked and stuff my fridge and cupboard with them so they would be available at any time I felt like eating them. Now this was hard for me to do, as I was scared that if I kept my favourite cookies at home I would end up eating the whole box soon or I would keep thinking about it and it would make me feel uncomfortable. That was the point really. I was supposed to allow myself to eat all this anytime I liked! The thought of having all this food at home was quite scary to me but I understood the logic of it. I wasn't ready to do it as yet but I did at least take the first step and promised myself I would never ever diet again.

At the same time my sister mentioned a psychoanalyst based in Brno who specialized in eating disorders. Two days later I went to see him. He listened to what I had to say, made lots of notes and asked me some questions. An hour later he looked at his watch and said, 'That will be all for today.'

I got up, paid the fee and left feeling intrigued. I could have gone for confession instead and it would have been free! But I found myself booking one more session with him for that week. The second session with him went similarly but as I was reading the books at the same time and thinking things through in a clear-headed fashion, I felt I made huge progress in my understanding of myself. By the end of that session it became clear to me that the core issue was dieting. So as long as I never went on a diet again, and focused instead on loving myself and loving food, I would be fine. The rest would follow, and it did.

However it is a longish process and even though you may progress very fast, eating disorders, or any addiction for that matter, take years to heal. And it is a continuous effort. For me the journey is even more challenging as I am still part of the glamour industry so while I tell myself that what matters the most is my health and my own love for myself and accepting my body for the way it is, whenever I am on an assignment, the work itself tells me the opposite. It focuses on the way the body looks and makes me conscious again. Sometimes I think it would be much easier for me if I just gave up this work altogether as I know that the day I do that I will be free of any internal struggle with food and my body. But well, it's a bigger challenge to be in this profession and thanks to that I have learned so much. So it's all for the good.

The thing with eating disorders or any unhealthy relationships with food is that you don't ever completely get over it. It takes years of normal eating and years of accepting and loving yourself till you get to the point where you don't think about food so much or worry about it in any way. Even now I can never consider food to be just food. For me it's always either unhealthy food, or fattening food or healthy food. It's never just food. I cannot eat a piece of white bread sandwich and not think, hey it's white bread! Watch out! Don't eat too much of it okay? This is what will go on in my head. It's in my DNA now and it will take me years to unlearn this internal dialogue of mine, this continuous judgement and there is a chance I will never be able to get rid of it totally. It is the same with my body. While I am much more relaxed about my body shape now, I still have to make a conscious effort not to judge my body as much and just love it the way it is. Even now I often find myself pulling my stomach in. It is like a reflex and I have to tell myself not to do it, but I often forget.

Where am I now

I used to think I was fearless. I used to be proud of it too, as I could do any adventure sports, sky diving, scuba diving, bungee jumping and I never felt a bit scared. Even when I did the TV show *Khatron Ke Khiladi* (the desi *Fear Factor*) I was never afraid to do any of the stunts. Then I realized there was something I actually did fear: food.

Some food was of course scarier than others but the scariest of them all was bread. It was scary because I loved it. I loved it so much that if I ate it I would lose all control whatsoever. So I avoided bread as much as possible to the point where if it were brought to my table in a restaurant, I would ask the waiter to remove it. I suppose bread was the lover I could never have and that made me long for him even more.

That is why I am truly in heaven now as for the first time in my life, my lover and I are finally united. Yes my friends, I am happy to announce that bread and I have made peace and I am officially not scared of him (it). And we make love every day! Yes! It is unbelievable I tell you! When you accept someone with all the good and bad, true love can grow. And I accept my beloved bread for its bad personality traits (it is after all refined flour with very little nutrients, can cause constipation and can make you gain weight) but I also see the good aspects of it, which is that it makes me feel happy and loved. Why loved? Because every time I allow myself to eat bread I am giving my body a message that says, 'I love you the way you are. You don't need to lose weight or be scared to put on weight. You don't need to be beautiful or be like anyone else. You don't need to change and become "perfect" because you *are* already perfect. You are the home for my soul and I appreciate you. And I will always love you even if you have a biiiig belly.'

I make sure that when I eat bread I eat it consciously; in other words, I try to be as present as possible, paying attention to every bite, its colour, the smell, the temperature, the taste. And at times, thanks to giving all my love to the process of eating and to my body, I do feel loved back by the food. I've had some funny experiences with this as well; for example, the first time I allowed myself to have my favourite duck and dumplings.

My boyfriend and I had just landed at the airport in Prague and as we were hungry and had nowhere to rush to, we decided to have a meal at a traditional Czech restaurant right there at the airport. This restaurant is by the way amazing as they serve the most popular Czech foods and they are just superb. We ate there once before but I had just a soup so it was my boyfriend who insisted we eat there as he loved the goulash there last time.

They had my duck on the menu so I got really excited and ordered it. Ten minutes later the duck was sitting in front of me. Oh I can't tell you, it was the most handsome duck ever. I had already psyched myself not to feel bad about all the fat in it but to give it all my love and enjoy it. No feeling of guilt whatsoever, but only acceptance! And with that I started eating.

Now the duck was of course delicious, simply blissful. But it was nothing in comparison to what I felt afterwards. When I finished it, I closed my eyes for a while and just kind of felt at one with the duck (dear reader, please don't laugh). As

I sat there with my eyes closed—my boyfriend was making his way through his goulash—I suddenly started feeling a tingling sensation in my hands and feet which slowly spread all over my body. It felt as if all the cells of my body had suddenly started giggling! I felt a wave of intense happiness and relaxation and began to giggle a little. My boyfriend wondered what was going on but I wasn't capable of describing it in words apart from saying, 'I feel like all the cells inside me are laughing!' And I laughed with them.

I have had a few more experiences like it since then. Perhaps not as intense, but very pleasant, giving me that happy giggling sensation as well. I get this mainly when I eat something I never used to (like bread) or when I eat foods I used to eat in my childhood. Cuckoo says that it is very good for us to sometimes eat the food we used to eat as children as it's part of our DNA so it's healthy for the body. And even though I felt no interest in eating meats such as pork or beef, I decided to try them the next time I was in Czech and so I did. I had some sausages and there was something about it for sure. I did feel as if I was reconnecting with my own self. Like getting in touch with some part inside me that was hidden and forgotten.

Food for me now is a way of loving myself. And the amazing thing is, the more you love yourself, the less attracted you are to unhealthy foods. That's just how it works. For years I would push myself into eating healthy all the time and that's when I desired the junk but now when I feel I have a choice and I don't *have to* eat healthy if I don't want to, I really *do want to* eat healthy most of the time! It again makes me feel more loved!

I have come to the conclusion that we are attracted to junk foods only when we don't really love ourselves that much. Or when we are guided by our minds and the knowledge we get from books about nutrition and when we restrain ourselves. When you don't do any of this, when there is no guilt, when there is no good and bad, but just food that you enjoy and food that you don't enjoy, you will see that the more love and care you feel for yourself, the more you will start getting attracted to healthy foods. So what you really need to do is not to focus on eating healthy but on loving yourself. And the rest will just follow.

It's been a very long journey for me. A journey that can never come to an end while I reside in this body as there is always more to learn. Initially my interest in food and fitness may have been fuelled by superficial reasons such as looking good, but today my understanding has changed 180° and my focus is on my health and feeling joyful and relaxed rather than getting a 'perfect' body with zero fat level.

So here I am, ready to share all I have learned with you. Now, before we start, remember to always be patient with yourself and whatever changes towards a healthier lifestyle you choose to make, do it slowly and peacefully. Never push yourself. There is no need to become a superhuman by tomorrow. Remember that it took me some ten years to arrive at this understanding that I will be sharing with you, so give yourself time as well and mainly, focus on the love.

Part 2

How to Get the Body You Love

In this section, I have focused on a balanced way of eating and exercising to achieve health and feel strong, vibrant and positive rather than obsessing about our body shapes. I believe that health and the way you feel inside your body and inside your mind are more important than being size zero. You need to do some mental reprogramming first, and so I have begun this section asking you to introspect a little about how you eat. However I will not disappoint those of you who have picked up this book for guidance on losing weight, because I know that it is easy for me to tell you, 'You know, just love yourself the way you are and don't worry about the extra kilos!' The fact is, if you are not ready to accept your body the way it is, you are just not ready. It's not easy to love the fat, I know it damn well. You can read a thousand books that keep telling you, 'Hey it shouldn't matter how you look, the real beauty is inside', and you will agree with all of it but, at the end of the day, when you look at yourself in the mirror and see that your waistline doesn't exist and the inside of your thighs are touching, all you'll be thinking is: 'Please god, help me lose some weight. Please! At least one kilo! I want to have a waist!'

It's not easy to accept your body shape just like that, in one moment when your whole life you have believed you need to be fitter. It is not and unfortunately it doesn't happen just because you have decided on it in this moment. You need to do some mind digging and reprogramming first, which will take a little time. But I understand you want to find some relief

59

immediately. I used to buy all the diet books and read them cover to cover in a day or two, impatient to know what I could do to lose weight RIGHT NOW. So I know how it is.

We all need to believe that we can also lose the weight, even though we understand that loving and accepting our body the way it is, is more important. That's why, even though I no longer believe in the concept of weight loss (for beauty), I shall give you all the tips you need right here. Just please make sure you take it slow and easy.

My motto (the outcome of my journey)

After having an unhealthy relationship with food and my body for more than seventeen years, suffering from an eating disorder, dieting, starving and over-exercising, I have come to a conclusion:

EATING SHOULD BE A CELEBRATION

Therefore the mottos I go with are:

1) *First feed your soul, then feed your body.*

2) *Whatever you do, do it not because you 'should' but because you 'want to'.*

As my teacher Cuckoo says (like many spiritual teachers) most of the diseases people suffer from today are caused by the mind. Hence, if you make yourself unhappy in any way, thinking negative thoughts or keeping unresolved negative emotions locked inside you, your body will react to it by creating a disease. The mind is where it all begins. Therefore, I'd rather first feed my soul with food I love and make myself happy than restrain myself from eating the foods I love and make myself unhappy. But, of course, the problem is that we often like food that isn't too good for us, don't we? So the question is one of balance. You should eat the food you love without any guilt even if you know it's not healthy, but at the same time you don't need me to tell you that eating high-sugar, high-fat foods all the time can't be good for you.

So we have a task.

How do we make ourselves LOVE the food that our body also LOVES?

The second task is to find a simple, no-fuss formula for eating right where we don't have to think too much. If there has been one positive outcome from my years of bad eating and over-dieting, it is this: I have learnt a lot about nutrition, diets and, most importantly, what works and what doesn't. I have finally come to my own very simple principles of eating well, which have to do with picking the right foods and the right quantities. And I will share these facts with you in the following pages. But before that, let's look at why it is that we fall into unhealthy patterns of eating in the first place.

Why we eat junk food

If you have learnt anything from my story in part one, it should be this: our relationship with food begins in our heads, not in our mouth or with our taste buds. This is what I will keep emphasizing through this book. So let's first look at why we eat badly in the first place. To understand this, you need to know the difference between real and emotional hunger, and why we are attached to certain foods.

Emotional hunger vs real hunger

Ask yourself the following questions:

- Do you often eat without realizing you're even doing it?

- Do you often find yourself eating when you are not hungry?
- Do you tend to eat junk foods when you are stressed, depressed or angry?
- Do you often overeat?
- Do you often gulp food down so quickly that you don't even know how much you ate?
- Do you use food to reward yourself?
- Do you sometimes find it hard to stop eating until you are too full?
- Do you feel food helps you to deal with your feelings?
- Do you find yourself thinking of food even when you're not hungry?
- Do you forbid yourself certain foods and feel guilty after eating them?
- Do you separate foods into good and bad according to how fattening they are?
- Are you often afraid of putting on weight after you have eaten something high in calories?

If you have answered yes to most of these questions, it's time you gave deeper thought to your relationship with food. One of the main causes of overeating is psychological, and understanding this is the key to overcoming food issues. Before you begin your journey towards fitness, it is important to realize exactly how you perceive eating and the food you consume. This will determine how easy or difficult it may be for you to alter your eating habits.

How do you go about this? First, you need to learn to distinguish between 'emotional' hunger and 'real' hunger, and to find an internal balance that you can maintain. Emotional eating is eating in response to your feelings without really feeling hungry. It means your emotions dictate when, what or how much you eat. Emotional eating is generally a form of escape. Many of us use food as a form of comfort (or consolation) when we are facing difficult situations in life. It's quite natural to do that, and *it is okay*, as long as it doesn't happen too often.

With the stressful lives we lead nowadays, it is natural to sometimes feel the need to comfort our souls with treats. It takes our mind away from the stress just for a moment, and you should allow yourself to do that when you really need to. Just be loving towards yourself and don't worry about it too much. You know, at times when you feel you need a hug and there is no one else to give you that hug, I think it's okay to get hugged by a little chocolate brownie, what say? :-)

I would never have allowed myself to do that before, and only I know how rigid, cold and unloving it felt inside my mind and my body during those times. So don't do that to yourself. It's okay to feel weak sometimes and succumb to eating junk food. Just accept it with love and compassion for yourself—if it is the feeling of ice cream melting in your mouth that will make you feel good for just a moment, then allow yourself the pleasure. Feeding yourself is a way of showing love for yourself and it is a deeply encoded message we carry inside us from the time when our mothers fed us as children, so when you restrain yourself from eating, on a subconscious level, you are giving yourself a message that you are not worth loving.

However, if you eat to satisfy your *emotional* hunger rather than your *physical* hunger too often and you feel you are not in control of it, then you may have a problem just as I did. This is technically called emotional eating (or compulsive eating), and it can develop into an actual eating disorder, which can be difficult to tackle. So treating yourself to a slice of cheesecake when you need some extra pampering is okay, but you should also make sure you enjoy eating it bit by bit because gulping it down without even realizing it is the first sign of something going wrong. And if you do this often (and unconsciously) it will sooner or later become a pattern, a habit, and well, you know, habits are damn hard to unlearn later. Emotional eating has become an issue for many people nowadays and it will remain an issue until we learn to face the worries and anxieties we carry inside us instead of trying to suppress them. And I agree it's not always that easy. It's hard work really.

Have you ever fallen in love and then lost some weight just because you didn't feel like eating that much? Love or any strong positive emotion can kind of fill you up in such a way that you will feel less physical hunger. The opposite is true as well. Feeling any void in your life can make you want to eat more. Some people gain lots of weight after experiencing a break-up (especially when they were not the ones making the call).

Once you have an inclination towards emotional eating, it will always be easy for your friends to tell if you are happy or not, just by looking at you and your weight fluctuations. I always lose weight when I fall in love as I start eating less (and stop bingeing altogether) as I feel I don't need food at all. The love fills me up. But when I am not in a relationship and I feel lonely, or I am stuck in a bad one, I gain weight right away. Recently I realized it wasn't about being in relationship. I just needed to fill that void inside me, and if love wasn't there to fill it, I would fill it with food. When I understood that all I was trying to do was to fill the emptiness I asked myself, why do I feel empty anyway? And then I saw how it was connected to feeling uninspired by my work. That was why I was empty. To be happy, I needed to be creative. And so what did fill that emptiness of mine? Songs. My own songs that is, made up of my words and feelings. And whenever I would sing them I would feel alive, real and happy. And the emptiness was gone.

So if you feel you may be suffering from an emotional eating problem in any measure, stop for a moment and think.

- What is it that makes me desire junk food or overeat?
- What is it that makes me drink, smoke or abuse my body in any way?
- Why am I feeling like this?
- What is there inside me that I'm trying to avoid feeling?
- What am I trying to escape from?

Finding these answers may take some time, but asking is what matters. The seeking, wanting to know, paying attention to yourself and doubting your own thoughts is important too, as we often end up lying to ourselves or just escaping the uncomfortable thoughts altogether.

So whenever you are about to poke into the fridge when you are not even hungry, pause for a moment, take a breath or two and just think first:

- Am I feeling real hunger or is this something else?
- What am I feeling right now?
- Am I feeling sad or upset or disturbed in any other way?
- What was I thinking before I started thinking of food?

- Did anything happen just now that made me feel bad in any way?
- Do I not enjoy what I was doing right now?
- Am I anxious or worried about something that might happen today or in the near future?
- What was the last thought I had before I decided to check out the fridge?

You may not always be able to tell exactly what's going on with you but sooner or later you will be able to differentiate the feeling of real hunger from feelings of boredom, sadness, anger and so on. In fact I'd say you should try not to eat immediately after any disturbing situation. Sit down, or have a cup of tea first; be with yourself, and when you are totally okay only then eat.

Our feelings can't be healed by food. Food only covers them up temporarily. The feelings will still be there, so using food is really only a distraction in the moment. This is what I have learnt. Each of us will have our own answers. Ultimately, I figured out that the root of my eating disorder wasn't my love for food. It was the emptiness I felt. And while I was scared of it and blamed it, food was not the actual problem. It never is! Food is healthful and delicious and meant to be enjoyed. It is your inability to deal with life's stresses and your negative emotions, an inability which you use food to suppress that are the issue.

Why we like unhealthy foods

'I wish I could like steamed veggies instead of bread pakoras,' a friend once sighed to me in despair. One of the reasons we might be eating unhealthily, as I have tried to show above, is that we are actually eating through our emotions.

The other more simple explanation is that we're just often attracted to the high-fat, high-sugar things. So let's ask the big question. Why?

Because it tastes 'good'

Our taste buds are used to high-fat, high-sugar foods, so when we eat something that is lower in sugar and fat, we don't find it as tasty.

Because they provide emotional comfort

These foods make your blood sugar rise, which gives you a temporary emotional/physical boost. This feeling becomes addictive.

Because it's a habit

We are often too lazy to step out of our comfort zones and spend the little free time we have on cooking or shopping for healthy foods that may not be easily available. Breaking any habit requires an effort; you will do it only if you believe it's worth it.

Because it's in our genes

Some sources say that eating these foods is in our genes, the reason being that early in our evolutionary history food was not very abundant. People who ate plenty of fatty or sugary foods (including carbohydrates) increased their adipose (fat) tissues, allowing them to survive longer during periods of low food supply. Since they survived longer, they reproduced more, and their offspring also had a taste for high-fat/sugar foods.

Because of all the brainwashing

How many times during a TV movie will you see the same ads repeated? Now let's say there is an ad for a burger that has come on about five times through the film. Your taste buds come to life just by seeing how juicy the burger looks as they fry it, the sauce that overflows, the cheese that melts so deliciously. Don't you want it right now?

Because we crave it

Some of our cravings are created by our minds or emotions. However, most of them are really just physical symptoms caused by hormones, fluctuations in blood sugar or the need for certain minerals or specific nutrients. Cravings can also be due to food allergies, candidiasis or PMS. For example, craving sweets is often caused by a deficiency of the mineral chromium. Also, cravings for salty foods can be a sign of weakened adrenal glands and your need for organic sodium, potassium and magnesium, while craving chocolate during PMS may be a sign of vitamin B deficiency. There is another way to deal with cravings. Start using supplements that are made of real food (I wouldn't recommend the chemically created ones) that are linked to the foods you are craving. You can do a search on Google or check with a doctor. In the index, you will find some Internet sites that provide great supplements of high quality.

What to do about it

Now that we know why our taste buds love these foods, let's go a little deeper and see if we can untangle our attachments to them. As I said earlier, it all begins in the mind. Now, our minds love being busy thinking at all times, and they love giving importance to things that don't matter much. So we often think of food more than is required. Our minds might even build it up to such an extent that food becomes such a heavenly treat that it ultimately becomes a hundred times better than the real thing.

Let me give you an example. I used to dream about this particular pizza I once had at a pizza joint in Mumbai. It was very, very thin and had tons of veggies on it, but mainly it was covered with four types of cheese. At the time I was trying to lose weight and pizza was a forbidden food, at least for a few months. But I was dying to have it again. So I often thought of it as a treat I would have when I lost all the weight I wanted to. The longer I was on that damn diet, the more I thought of that pizza and fantasized about it.

Now guess what happened when I finally ate the pizza again? Do you think it satisfied me as much as I had imagined it would? Was I in heaven eating it just as I thought I would be? No! I wasn't! How come? Well, guess what, the pizza didn't taste as good anymore! At first I thought they must have done it differently, perhaps fired the old chef or changed the recipe. But hey, this was a pizza chain, and these guys don't change their recipes for years, once the pizza becomes popular, do they?

That's when I realized that I had made this pizza into my ultimate food dream, a little pizza god that I worshipped. And with time my mind added a few extra colours to this picture. So now this ordinary pizza turned into a superhero-pizza in my head, which of course was far better than the reality! How do you beat that? You just can't!

This just shows how powerful our minds are. They can turn anything into something else. The other way to look at it is that the love that we feel for a particular food is not wholly connected to the food itself. Food always tastes better in our minds that on our palates and if we recognize that, we're one step along the way to detaching ourselves from our bad habits.

Think for example about the fact that often our memories of having a really good meal have other memories attached to them—remember the time you were starving on that road trip and the plateful of rice and dal that you were served in that little dhaba seemed better than any biryani? You still remember it don't you? Or that memorable birthday meal with friends and family where the table groaned with food. The food you ate may have been genuinely tasty, but invested with your great memories, it becomes tastier still.

So watch out for the mind's tricks, okay? And if you ever think it will be hard for you to start eating healthier, believe me, as long as you want to and you give yourself time to get used to the changes, it will happen, even if you don't like eating veggies and love sugary treats instead.

Clearing your taste buds

The simplest way to retrain your taste buds is for you to limit unnatural foods, such as soft drinks, deep-fried foods, artificial sweeteners, or addictive foods, like coffee and sugar, from your diet. In fact I only have one food rule. Eat natural foods, anything you like, and limit three things as much as possible: sugar, deep-fried foods and soft drinks. These foods numb the body with their strong flavours and chemicals and when you limit them, you will start enjoying the taste of natural things. And of the three, I would ask you to cut the soft drinks first. I will gladly eat two huge slices of a cake dripping with chocolate, which may pretty much equal the amount of calories (and sugar) that a Coke has, but at least it's real food, not chemicals dissolved in liquid. Of course, giving up our old habits is easier said than done. Sugar for example is super addictive, and it is an addiction like any other to the extent that if you are a sugar addict and you go totally off it suddenly, you will quite likely experience withdrawal symptoms (headaches, nausea, flu-like symptoms, fatigue, depression and moodiness). Some experts say that you need to give a child a new food something like fifteen to twenty times before they will develop a taste for it. I wouldn't be surprised if it was as difficult for some adults.

Take small steps

You need to be gentle with yourself. It took me years to get to where I am; it might take you a while too. You don't need to start eating salads from tomorrow, you know. Eat healthy whenever you feel like and feel good about it. Start with eating a side salad or some veggies on the side with your meals even if you are starting with just one tomato. That's no effort at all and once it becomes a habit, it will all become easier for you. There is no need to try to eat a huge salad instead of your usual meal. Have both and enjoy! Loving and enjoying your food is the most important thing; we certainly don't want you to suffer eating just a salad.

Make up little challenges for yourself

Give yourself a small time frame in the beginning so you goal seems achievable and not such a big deal. It may be too much to start by saying, 'Okay I won't have sugar for thirty days', only to realize a few days later that it bothers you. Then the challenge will turn into a negative experience and sooner or later you will be fed up with it, give in to the temptation and only end up feeling bad at the end of it. So start by deciding to do one sugar-free day instead of saying you will go off sugar for a month!

Find substitutes that you enjoy

Try replacing sweets with your favourite fruit. I love to suck on pineapple after meals at times. Even though it's generally said that fruits should be eaten on an empty stomach, I'd rather have the pineapple than dessert. Or if I feel I really need something much sweeter, I'll make tea with lots of honey. That satisfies me for sure—generally, by the time I have half the cup, I feel satisfied.

Improve the way you eat

At this point, I think you have some tools to assess how and why you eat the way you do. Now you need to make a change, and, as we go further along this chapter, I'll spell out the basic principles of eating right. But before I do that, I want you to prepare yourself to eat right. And the only way you can do that is by being constantly aware of how you eat and how your body reacts to the food you're consuming.

My six principles for how to eat

I manage my eating by following six very simple principles.

Eat when your body tells you it's ready

It's important to follow your body's signals and eat when your body requires it. This means that when you start feeling slight hunger pangs, it's a signal that you should eat *right now*. This way you avoid your blood sugar levels dropping, causing fluctuating energy levels, mood swings and cravings. As the body is then prepared to eat, the food will be digested and absorbed much better and all the nutrients utilized more efficiently. However, if you eat when you're not hungry, your body may not be ready to deal with new food coming in as yet, which results in weight gain. When you follow the eating plan I suggest in this book, you will be getting slightly hungry just when it's time to have your next meal. That way you will also enjoy the food much more, as everything tastes so much better when we're hungry, doesn't it?

Eat with awareness

Do you ever finish your meal without even realizing what exactly was on your plate? This is often the case if you eat while watching TV, making phone calls or just lost in your thoughts. What happens then is that your body doesn't really get the chance to register it's been fed and then, naturally, you may overeat. So make sure you really *eat* when you eat. Enjoy your food thoroughly, giving it your full attention. This way you will feel more satisfied as well.

Eat slowly and chew properly

The more you chew, the easier it is for your stomach to digest the meal and absorb the nutrients, simply because big pieces of food take longer to break down and require more energy output from your stomach, which results in less energy for you to use! The act of chewing also produces digestive enzymes in your saliva which then get mixed with the food in your mouth, helping to digest it. Also, it takes time for your body to register that it's satiated, so when you eat too fast, you may eat more than you need to as the feeling of 'fullness' takes time to register.

Don't eat when you're stressed or on the run

If you eat on the run or when you're stressed you are also stressing your internal organs and may develop indigestion, heartburn and trapped air. Do you think your body can function well like that? Of course not! Research shows that eating when you're stressed creates acidity in your system. An acidic environment is the perfect environment for various diseases to develop, by the way. So pause for a moment when you're about to eat. And if you're feeling stressed, just take a minute first, close your eyes and take a few deep breaths . . . and only then eat.

Don't skip meals

Many of us have the habit of skipping meals (usually breakfast) without realizing that the longer you stay on an empty stomach, the lower your blood sugar level drops, which increases cravings and lowers energy levels. When that happens, it's extremely hard to control what you eat at your next meal, however strong your willpower. Your body will simply take over, making you grab some sugary carbs in an effort to raise the blood sugar quickly. If you want to get in shape you will have to stop skipping meals, because the more frequently you eat, the better control you will have over *what* you eat.

Treat your food with respect

There are people out there who have nothing to eat. So even if the food doesn't taste as good as you wish, or even if it's 'junk food' and you think you shouldn't be eating such things at all, still, feel grateful that you *have* this food on your plate, and eat it with respect and gratitude.

Learn to listen to your body

Listen to your body and make it your teacher. This is one of the big lessons Cuckoo taught me. By that I mean your body should be the first voice you always listen to, before you listen to anyone else, however authoritative that person may be. See, we are all different and we all have different bodies. We live in different conditions; we have different lifestyles, different ages, different genetics and so on. Our bodies also react differently to various foods, so while some of us may be allergic to a particular food, others may be totally fine with it or even thrive on it.

This is important, especially when reading books on diets or food, as whatever the author suggests may certainly be great for a lot of people out there but not necessarily for everyone. Now this may sound strange coming from me as I will soon be recommending certain diet alterations and it sounds as if I were saying you shouldn't really trust what you read in this book either, doesn't it?

The thing is, there are certain basic guidelines that are good for everyone. Like, if I say please stay away from soft drinks and deep-fried food, I think it's quite clear that, whatever body type you have, there is no way these could be good for you. However if I said, for example, that you should drink watermelon juice every morning, it may not be a great idea for those who require warmer and heavier foods according to ayurveda, such as people with a dominant vata constitution.

So this is why I say that first of all you need to listen to your own body and follow what it says. It's as simple as don't have a cold drink if you are feeling cold. That's common sense right? Yet we do these things. Sometimes it's not as simple though, so you need to really pay attention to your body. It's kind of like trying to discover your body's 'code', like a secret number combination for a safe-deposit box. The code for each of us is unique; knowing it means totally understanding yourself and your body. For example, this means knowing which foods are good for you and which are not, what kind of lifestyle suits you and makes you feel in balance, how much physical activity is good for you, how much stress or strain you can take, how much sleep you need and so on. It's simply knowing how to take care of your body in the best possible way at all times.

In order to get to know this 'code' you need to decode the language of your body and become familiar with it. It's a trial-and-error approach really, but this is how you learn.

So how do you do it? How can you start hearing this inner voice of your body?

First become sensitive to how it feels to 'be *inside* your body' at all times. We often forget to be conscious of how we feel as we keep running through the whole day, without stopping and just '*being in*' the body. So for starters I'd say that, during your busy day, just take a pause sometimes, sit down if you can, take a few deep breaths for a while and observe how you feel in all the parts of your body. Then ask yourself a few questions to check how your body is doing. Are you feeling any tension anywhere? Can you breathe deeply and relax a bit more? Stretch a little, align your back, massage your hands or your neck and mainly just breathe. Do this especially if you feel you have been too busy the whole day to give your body any attention. Find this little time for yourself several times a day.

Another good tip is to just sit down and look at nature. Even if it is just one little plant in a pot that you have at home. Looking at nature will always relax you, first because the colour green has a calming effect and second because nature (flora and fauna both) is in the 'present moment'. It just 'exists'. And to just simply be without trying to *be* is immensely peaceful and relaxing and joyous. So when you look at plants, the feeling of peace kind of rubs off on you a little. When you are in the midst of a busy day and you suddenly realize you hardly know where you are (office, or walking on the street) as you are so immersed in your work, just take a little break, sit for a while and look at the sky or a bird that is hopping around. Immediately you will feel more 'here'. And when you feel more 'here' you will automatically feel more 'inside' your body.

You should be doing the same with your mind, as your mental state directly affects your health. In other words, whatever you think and feel during the day causes energy shifts in your body, so if you think negative thoughts, or are stressed and unhappy, it's not just your mind that deals with it but your entire body. To give you a simple example, remember how it feels when you get upset with someone. I'm sure you have noticed in the past how negative feelings can cause your stomach to tense up and your breath to become shallow. If you keep thinking these negative thoughts for a long period of time it's even possible to experience indigestion, or get acidity, right?

However, if you change the direction of your thoughts and start thinking of something nice, such as your beloved and the romantic times you have spent together, your breath will deepen again and your muscles will loosen up. The tension will then go away, right? Now all these feelings cause energy waves that go through your body and affect the functioning of your internal organs. When this keeps happening repeatedly, such as when you go through difficult times in life dealing with various problems, relationship issues, or fears, the energy will stop flowing freely through your body (from one organ to another), which results in organ malfunction and, ultimately, disease. So watching your mind and being aware of the thoughts you create is essential to maintaining your health. Remember, in those moments when you stop for a while to give your body attention and check how it's doing, to check your mind and your feelings as well.

I also try and stay aware of how my stomach is doing especially after I have eaten. I check if the food feels light or heavy, if the digestion is going smoothly or not. This is how you can discover which foods are good for you and which ones are not. For example, I know that chicken is not good for me as whenever I eat it, I feel like it's sitting in my stomach like a brick. Unless I eat just a very tiny bit, I can't seem to be able to digest it easily. Or if I have more than half a glass of milk, I feel kind of 'sticky' inside.

It's also good to observe your energy levels after your meal. Have they gone down or up; are you feeling sleepy or full of energy? If you feel tired, it's obvious you have either eaten too much or you ate something that wasn't good for you. With every experience like this you can create a mental 'list' of 'yes' and 'no' foods for you, even though I would suggest you think of it more as 'very-good-for-me foods' and 'not-so-good-for-me foods', so you don't feel restrained or feel guilty if you have one of those 'no' foods.

Like for example, let's say you often get acidity, okay? What you should do is write down everything you ate that day or what you did and how you felt (stress can also cause acidity). The next time you get acidity, compare notes and look for connections. This is how you learn more about your body and the food you eat, and also learn to prevent sickness. Plus, you will also save money on doctor's fees!

Sometimes you may need to experiment and change your diet for a while, drop certain foods and notice if you feel better. And then, just to be sure, you can reintroduce them into your diet after a few weeks and see if the symptoms reappear. It's kind of a self study, a little detective work, and this is what I mean by saying discover the 'code' of your body.

Another message that your body gives you about its health is visual—the state of your skin, nails, hair, under-eye colour, colour of your eyes and your tongue and so on. If your skin is breaking out into pimples, it's obvious something or the other is out of balance. The skin is the biggest elimination organ of the body, so whatever toxins you carry inside, your body will try to get rid of them by throwing them out through your skin. However, just to remind you, while most of the time your skin problems are related to diet, it may not be just your diet that is responsible, but the state of your mind. (See, it always goes back to that, doesn't it?)

I recently went through a break-up and it hurt me a lot. In fact, I can say I have never felt so much pain (I even felt it as a physical pain in my chest), so much so that I developed these boils on one side of my forehead. I also got a huge white spot under one of my nails on the left hand and when I showed it to Cuckoo he told me this was due to stress, as the spot appeared in the nervous system meridian. I wasn't surprised at all to hear that.

How to find out what food is good for your body

Drop a particular food group for two weeks and see how you feel. For example, totally stop all dairy products and monitor your energy levels day by day, the appearance of your skin and the overall feeling in your body. After the first week you will be able to see a difference for sure. But I'd suggest you continue for one more week just to be sure. After the second week has passed and you have noted the difference it made to your body, reintroduce this food into your diet and again notice how you feel. THEN you will be able to tell for sure if this food is good for your body or not!

In most cases, when people do this test with dairy products, they experience amazing changes in their level of energy and health after dropping dairy.

Those who suffer from allergies or running nose and cough suddenly realize it was the dairy products that caused this because, after a few days, they are totally free of all the symptoms. Eliminating one particular food group for a while and then reintroducing it into your diet will give you very clear signals whether it is good for you to eat or not. Your body becomes more sensitive and you'll be able to feel the actual impact of this food item on your body.

It's good to try these tests with foods that you just know are not good for you because until you drop them totally, you won't be able to feel their effect on you as your body is used to being 'drugged' by them. I have tried this several times with coffee. I used to have a few cups of coffee every day; I simply loved the taste of coffee. Then one day I decided to get rid of my addiction and have no coffee for at least two weeks. Guess what happened two weeks later when I had a cup? With my first sip I felt this strange feeling in my brain, as if something chemical was attacking my brain. Then I got high, but soon after that I experienced a sudden drop of energy and I started feeling extremely dehydrated. I was SO dehydrated that I drank like six litres of water in the next five hours. And I felt extremely uncomfortable. Interestingly, however, if I start drinking coffee regularly again, my body quickly adapts and I feel all right with it again. So this is coffee for me.

If there are any foods that you suspect are bad for you, try going off them for two weeks and then eating (drinking) them again; your body will give you a clear message if they are good for you or not.

Learning to eat right

Now it's time to come to the meat, so to speak. Before we talk about how to eat right in order to get and stay in shape, I need to first emphasize how important it is to just simply 'eat'. What I mean to say is, if you go on a depriving diet that makes you eat less or cut out a macronutrient altogether, it won't help you to get into shape in the long run. In fact, as the experienced and compulsive diet-o-holic that I used to be, I can tell you:

> If you want to lose weight permanently, dieting is the worst thing you can do.

Now this is good news for you, because now you don't need to worry that what you will read further will be some 'how to starve yourself real good' tips. Oh no! We are going to do just the opposite. We are going to EAT! And we are going to eat ourselves to health and to fitness! Yes! You will even get to know how you can shape your body and transform yoursel into a super fit human by . . . yes! EATING! That doesn't sound bad at all, does it?

You ready? Positive? Excited?

I am!

So let's go for it!

Now, I would like to start by giving you some useful information about how our bodies work and how food 'works' inside our bodies, because knowing this will give you lots of clues on why your body reacts the way it does when you eat a particular thing. With this understanding, you will then be able to choose what you eat more responsibly as you will know the consequences. Just that. Simple. And then you will become your own nutritionist if you wish to, and, I tell you, it is much better that way.

See, what works the best in life in general is following yourself rather than following someone else. It's like that with everything. Following someone else often makes us do stupid things, or at least things that we simply shouldn't do because it is not 'us', not our own way, not our own path. Cuckoo always says the problem is that people always prefer to follow someone else (someone they consider authoritative) rather than to follow themselves. He says, 'I point my finger at the moon but people don't look at the moon! They look at my finger!'

I'm saying this now because I also want to make sure once again that you follow your own self before you take advice from anyone else, be it doctors, teachers or this book. So while a lot of the following is information that was proved by science (and science surely doesn't know it all, far from it) and tested by many, it doesn't necessarily mean that it is the ultimate truth or that it should become the 'truth' for you. In fact never ever take anything as the ultimate truth. Experience it first, and see if it resonates with you, if it seems to be working for your body and if it makes logical sense to you. As it is with all books, whatever is written here is only the truth of the author.

Over the years, I have read lots of diet, nutrition, health and fitness books, I have googled and googled; I have hired personal trainers and travelled the world attending workshops, retreats and classes all related to food, health and exercise. So all I can say is that this is what works for me the most. This is what makes me feel balanced, relaxed, healthier, more energetic and more positive. See if some of these tips could work for you too. And for the rest, just follow yourself! :-)

How food turns into energy

In order to understand how you should eat so your body thrives on all levels, you need to understand some basics about how your body absorbs food and turns it into energy. It's very simple actually, and once you know this, it will help you to understand how to eat, how much and how often. In fact, once you know these simple basics, you will read the rest of the book in agreement with everything I say, thinking, yeah I already know this, because it's logical! Now it's going to get a bit technical here but don't worry; I have simplified the information as much as possible so it is easier for you to 'digest' it.

All the food you eat is broken down in the digestive system into its various components or building blocks. Carbohydrates are broken down into single sugar units: glucose, fructose and galactose. Fats are broken down into fatty acids and proteins are broken down into amino acids.

Step 1: Digestion

When you take a bite and start chewing, the food gets covered in saliva, which contains enzymes for the digestion of carbohydrates. This is where the digestive process technically begins. Once you swallow, the food goes down and enters your stomach, where digestion continues. The digestive liquids in the stomach contain enzymes to digest proteins.

The time taken to finish digestion varies according to the quantities of carbohydrates, protein or fats present, since they all require different lengths of time to be digested. Also, the less you chew the food, the longer it takes to digest, as it takes longer for the stomach acids to get through big pieces.

Step 2: Glucose extraction

While the food is being digested, glucose (the simple sugar that is the fuel for the body) is extracted from the food and enters the bloodstream, where it circulates, waiting to be absorbed by cells. The cells absorb as much glucose as they need to supply immediate energy to the body. Each cell is limited in how much glucose it can absorb at a time, so when all the cells have been 'fed' and they become 'full', the rest of the glucose is redirected, with the help of the hormone insulin, into 'storage'.

A short note about insulin

Insulin is a hormone produced by the pancreas. It is absolutely essential because it helps glucose to pass through the walls of every cell so energy can be created. So insulin is pretty much like a watchman (guarding the walls of cells), and this watchman is the only one who has the key to the house, so, without him, no one can get in. Insulin regulates the amount of glucose in the blood, converts excess glucose into glycogen and helps excess glucose to be stored as fat.

The amount of insulin in the blood directly depends on the amount of glucose in the blood. The more you eat, the more insulin gets created so it can either assist the glucose to enter the cells or store the excess glucose elsewhere. It also means that the more insulin the body creates, the more glucose will be stored as fat, which is not great news is it?

Step 3: Glucose storage

The first 'storage' spaces for glucose are muscles and the liver. This is where glucose is stored in the form of glycogen so it can be easily withdrawn whenever required (it is short-term storage). This means that, after the glucose in cells is used up, the body will release glucose from muscles and the liver to serve as a new energy supply. However, if the storage space in muscles and the liver gets full, and there is still some glucose left to be stored, insulin will direct the remaining glucose into another 'storage space'.

Step 4: Fat storage

After the storage capacity in the muscles and liver gets filled, the remaining glucose gets stored in fat cells (both old and newly created ones). We, of course, want to prevent that from happening, right? So we need to make sure that it never gets to this point so no fat is ever stored! How do we do that? Simply by eating the right amount of food that will be just enough to supply our body with the necessary energy and not more than that. There is also one more thing that we can do, which is to *increase* the storage capacity of the muscles and the liver. We can do this by exercising. So if you exercise regularly, your body will not have as high a tendency to store fat as it would if you didn't exercise at all!

In the following sections I will teach you how to eat in such a way that this last step (storing of fat) can be avoided altogether. And this is really the key to eating right.

Eating right

One lesson we can take from what I've just said to you is that the key to eating right and not gaining weight is to eat in order to get a continuous supply of energy and never store it as fat. The trick is in eating frequent, smaller portions of food. Let's start with frequent eating.

Frequent eating

Most of us have been used to eating three times a day our whole life. It's not because it is healthy or for any other smart reason. It's just a habit. We often get hungry between meals, but instead of taking it as a signal that we should naturally be eating more often, we binge on unhealthy snacks till it's the time for the next meal.

By the time we are about to have another meal, we are so hungry that we grab anything front of us, forget being selective and thinking of healthy nutrition. It happens to me as well, however disciplined I am. This urgent hunger makes me overeat easily. If I get too hungry, I get totally cranky and want to gulp down the first thing I lay my eyes on.

Now if you recollect what you know about blood sugar levels, you can probably connect all the information together, and you won't need me to tell you why eating only three times a day won't do you any good. As we discussed before, we need to keep our blood sugar levels as stable as possible. Every time you get too hungry, your blood sugar levels plummet and your body starts screaming: 'Give me food! NOW!' Hence, the lower your blood sugar drops, the harder it is to control yourself and the first instinct is to grab some sugary carbohydrates.

Frequent eating is really the trick. It's not some great science but I can't tell you what a big difference it can make to your body and weight loss! The benefits of frequent eating are worth adjusting your lifestyle for so let me put them down again.

Frequent eating

- Helps the body to absorb and utilize nutrients better.
- Helps to spread out the calories throughout the day, hence there is less chance that the body will store it as fat (remember that all the excess calories from one meal will be stored as fat).
- Helps to speed up metabolism in the most effective way and therefore speed up calorie burning as well.
- Helps to prevent bingeing and cravings.
- Helps to maintain high energy levels throughout the day by regulating blood sugar and insulin levels.

When your body gets used to the fact that it is getting food every few hours, it will stop storing fat as it knows there is no starvation coming up soon. Also the more meals you eat in a day, the more consistently your metabolism gets a boost. Research shows an increase in the metabolic rate in your body for as long as five hours every time you eat.

Take the example of animals in the wild. Those who eat frequently (graze) have lean bodies (such as horses, elk, sheep) but look at bears. A bear eats a large quantity of food at one time and then goes for days or even months without eating at all. This way, its body stores the food energy as a huge amount of fat so it can survive for a long time without eating (in winters). When you provide your body with a regular supply of nutrients your metabolism speeds up, and you will have less hunger pangs and better control over what you eat. This is the right way to help your system create the right metabolic environment that supports fat loss and muscle gain.

I can't tell you how much it works!

I used to use the alarm on my phone to remind myself of my meal timings. I would set it for every 2.5 hours and when it buzzed I would take it as a cue to eat. I don't do that anymore, as I feel it's more important to listen to my body and take the cue from there—it also helps you to get more sensitive to your bodily signals. However, I would still recommend it to all of you who are not used to eating frequently or to those who get so busy during the day that they often forget to eat. Of course planning your meal does require some effort but I tell you, the benefits are worth it!

Let me give you an example of my own optimal meal timings.

Meal 1: 9.30 a.m.
Meal 2: 12.00 p.m.

Meal 3: 2.30 p.m.
Meal 4: 5.00 p.m.
Meal 5: 7.30 p.m.

Now, if I keep three hours in between, (which sometimes happens as I often get a bit delayed) I may end up eating the last meal a bit later (sometimes as late as 9 p.m.), which would generally not be the best but because I don't go to sleep before midnight on most days, it's okay; by the time I hit the bed, the food is digested. If I could have it my way, I wouldn't eat later than 8 p.m., but because of my work schedule, that's sometimes impossible. So it's all about making the best of what you have.

If there is a gap between meal 5 and bedtime, you will probably get hungry. I know I do. In case you get hungry late at night, the best thing you can have is a piece of fruit, a handful of nuts, a smoothie or soup. Liquid meals don't require much digestion.

Most fitness trainers will tell you not to have fruits or any other carbs at night. I quite agree with the fact that having carbohydrates at night is not the best, especially if you're trying to lose weight, as you don't end up using those calories. However, at the same time, I feel that if you're hungry an hour before going to bed, nothing will be digested as fast as fresh fruit. Fruits are generally digested within thirty minutes, apart from bananas and dried fruits, which may take up to forty-five minutes. So I tend to eat an apple if I am hungry before bed. Plus fresh fruit is not really going to make you put on weight, if you worry about that. I think what's more important is that your body won't be digesting while it needs to rest. So if you do eat very late at night, just have something that your stomach won't be working on while you sleep.

The fact is, if getting in shape is your goal, however hard you exercise, if you keep eating three square meals (even if they are nutritionally well balanced), you will never achieve as great results as you would if you were eating smaller meals five (or six) times a day. (Some professional athletes actually eat as many as seven to eight times a day!)

Eating the right portions

The next question is, of course, how much you should be eating during those five meals. If you eat five enormous meals then you're in trouble.

The portion is important, as all excess calories are stored as fat. So if you eat as frequently as I suggest (five to six times a day), all you need to do is to measure the size of the carbohydrate and protein portions according to the size and the thickness of your palm. It's that simple. So your plate will then have one portion of carbohydrates (size and thickness of your palm) and a portion of protein (again the size and thickness of your palm).

Now you will ask me, how do I know what is the size and thickness of my palm if I'm eating chicken curry or chappatis? With chicken curry, I would look at the size of the chicken pieces and compare them to my palm by just putting the chicken pieces all together on one side of the plate and then look at the amount and see that it kind of visually matches the size of my palm. As for chappatis, it's the same thing. You see the thickness and size of it and compare it to your palm and guess. There is no need to weigh something and be anal about it! One chappati is generally enough for one portion.

The rest of the plate you should fill with vegetables, and that you don't really need to measure. Why? Because even though vegetables are generally carbohydrates as well, they don't really add any calories to the meal, even if you have tons of them. In fact they have so-called *negative calories* as they use up more calories/energy to digest than the calories they actually contain! This gives vegetables a tremendous natural fat-burning advantage and that's why you can eat as many vegetables as you want. They will fill you up and provide lots of nutrients and fibre. Just remember that if the vegetables are cooked in lots of oil then, of course, they *will* add calories!

Now where did the portion of fat go? You definitely need to add a good fat to your meals, as fat is very important. However if your protein portion happens to be non-veg, then you don't need to add any extra fat as the fat is naturally already there. But if your protein option comes from a vegetarian source (for example dal, pulses or tofu), then you should add a tablespoon of good oil or a dressing to it.

And then, of course, see how you feel after you have eaten. If you still feel a bit hungry, have a few more bites. Once your body gets used to eating frequently you will also recognize what is the right feeling in your stomach (what is the right fullness) and that you need to stop eating once you get that feeling (once you feel satiated). The right fullness would be feeling satiated (and not hungry anymore) but not 'full'.

You will know with practice when to stop eating, and you will then understand what the right portion for you is with time. If you are hungrier earlier than your next mealtime (earlier than 2.5 hours after you ate last), it means you have not eaten enough, and you know the right portion for the next time. If you are not feeling hungry at all when your next mealtime comes, then you know you ate more than you needed at the previous meal, and so, the next time, you need to make the portion smaller. So you figure out the exact portions for your body as you go. That's where you need to be sensitive to the signals of your stomach again. Some of us have faster metabolisms, some of us slower, so follow your OWN stomach and not a food weighing machine.

A few examples of meals

Potato + fish + lightly cooked vegetables

Rice + dal + veggies in light gravy containing a spoon of sunflower oil

Turkey sandwich (with brown bread) + salad

Noodles + chicken + stir-fried veggies

Toast with butter +egg-white omelette + salad + a few nuts or seeds

Rice + tofu + stir-fried vegetables

These are simple examples of how to make one portion for yourself. Of course the portions for men and women differ, just as the size and thickness of our palms differ. That's why measuring a portion against a part of your own body is the best as we have different needs according to our body sizes.

Such meals will make you feel balanced and not crave anything further as all the macronutrients are present at once. And why should you eat all the macronutrients together? Protein and fat both slow down the digestion which means that, if you eat them together with a carbohydrate, you will be lowering the glycaemic index of the carbohydrates, in other words slowing down the release of glucose, which, as you already know, is important. Eating vegetables (that contain lots of fibre) will also help to slow down the digestion and therefore keep your blood sugar levels stable. Remember, non-fluctuating glucose and insulin levels will help the food to be used for energy rather than for fat storage.

However, please don't worry if you can't get your meal nutritionally well balanced like this every time. Sometimes it may not be possible and you don't necessarily have to do it every single meal. Yes, protein and fat will for slow down the release of glucose (from carbohydrates) into the bloodstream, but it's totally okay not to eat, for example, protein at every meal. You will not be protein deficient just because you don't eat protein at every meal. For example, I have porridge for breakfast and many of you might choose to have idli, dosa or muesli, or just toast. That's fine, especially in the morning as your blood sugar level is very low then (after the whole night of 'fasting') and you will also burn the carbohydrates anyway during the day.

What matters the most is that you eat smaller portions of meals throughout the day. If you want to lose some weight, that is the first thing you want to follow, eating small meals and eating frequently. What exactly it is you eat won't matter as much, as long as it's not full of sugar or full of oil. Just don't stress about it okay?

The great dabba trick

The key word is 'dabba'. My manager often tells me that I should endorse the brand Ziploc and I agree. I would be the best ambassador for them as I carry Ziploc dabbas wherever I go. This is my secret. I travel almost all the time, or go on locations to shoot and I tell you, if I can make it work with my hectic schedule, so can you.

In the morning, I put some porridge or muesli in the dabba and eat that on the flight later, instead of their oily or fried breakfast. At the hotel, I generally ask for some baked or grilled fish and tons of veggies or dal and rice, or lamb at times (less often) and if the hotel doesn't have my brown rice, I'll ask for a boiled or baked potato as that's definitely more nutritious than refined white rice. However, I'm not anal about it (not anymore, I used to be) so if I'm ordering Thai curry, I won't eat it with a potato!

I always ask for an extra plate of steamed vegetables, which I eat with soy sauce. It's delicious. When they send me the food, I split it into two portions, eat one and put the other one in my dabba and carry that with me to my rehearsals (I travel most of the time to do Bollywood dance performances at events).

So basically, the secret is the dabba. Whenever I get the chance to get healthy food, I put that in the dabba. So let's say I am at the airport in the lounge and they have some idlis in the lounge buffet, I pop that in my dabba as well. I may not be hungry at that time, so I will keep it in my dabba and eat it later on the flight. So if you have very little time to cook in a day, what you can do is carry your dabba and pick up healthier food somewhere on the way to work.

Macronutrients: a very quick survey

Now let's have a look at what are the best options of carbohydrates, protein and fat we should be having.

Carbohydrates

Carbohydrates are the primary source of energy for our body.
Without them you would feel continuously tired and moody
and crave sweets (which is what happens when you go on a
low-carb diet).

My experience with a low-carb diet

If you have ever tried a low-carbohydrate diet
(such as the infamous Atkins diet), you might have
initially thought that you had won the battle. For
the first two months, so did I. Then, as you know, it
backfired—badly! See, what happens when you eat
less carbohydrates is that your body doesn't get its
primary source of fuel and so it starts using the fat as
fuel, which means you start losing fat. However, apart
from fat, the body also starts using protein for fuel,
which means you will start losing muscle. This muscle
loss will result in a slowing down of the metabolism
which slows down weight loss as well.

In medical terms the process by which the body
converts fat to energy is called ketosis. When the body
undergoes ketosis for too long, it can change the acidity
of your blood, which is extremely harmful to your liver
and kidneys. Then what do you think happens when
you start eating carbohydrates again? In the long run,
your body eventually gets used to this state of ketosis
by changing the behaviour of the fat cells. The same
fat cells become much more active in their ability to
accumulate fat, which of course translates into very

quick weight gain. Another disadvantage is that even if you manage to stick to the diet for a long time, sooner or later you will hit a plateau and stop losing weight altogether (which happens anyway with all diets at some point).

Good carbs and not-so-good carbs

The *good* carbs are generally all carbohydrates that are in their natural state or as close to it as possible. For example, there is nothing wrong with sugar cane, but once it is processed and made into white sugar, it loses its nutritional value and becomes basically empty calories. Remember, processed foods significantly raise our blood sugar levels, which is ultimately what causes weight gain.

See, the more processing the carbohydrate goes through, the more fibre it loses. Fibre is the indigestible part of plant foods that functions as a broom in our intestines. Its main job is to keep the digestive tract clean. It also acts like a sponge, soaking up acids from the body. Fibre is very important, but when it's removed in the processing, it makes the carbohydrate break down (digest) much faster in the stomach, which ultimately affects our blood sugar levels negatively. So the *bad* carbs are carbs that used to be *good* once upon a time, but because we processed them, refined them and who knows what not, they've become unhealthy and 'fattening'. (I'd prefer not to use the word 'bad' or separate things into 'good' and 'bad' for the psychological reasons that I talked about before, however, in this context it is just easier to say 'bad' carbs rather than not-so-good-for-you carbs, right? So I'll use the word 'bad' here but just remember, you don't need to feel 'bad' when you eat the 'bad' carbs. Just choose the better carbs whenever you feel like and when you don't then don't. No pressure okay?)

It's like if you compare eating wholegrain bread to the white bread toast you generally get. Which one of them do you think will be digested faster? The white bread of course. If you eat the wholegrain bread, it will take you longer to chew as well, and just one slice will make you feel fuller, in comparison to eating one slice of white bread, right? You'll probably need to eat two slices of white bread toast just to give you the same feeling of fullness one slice of wholegrain bread would give you. It's the same thing if you compare eating a bowl of white rice and a bowl of brown rice. Brown rice, with its high fibre content, will take longer to break down than white rice.

Now the higher your blood sugar levels go, the more insulin is created by the body to handle all this traffic. And as insulin is a storage hormone, the more insulin that's created, the more glucose will be stored as fat. We don't really want this to happen, right? Plus there are other things that are also happening. Once your blood sugar levels spike and insulin brings the blood sugar down again you experience a drop in energy. So you go through these ups and downs in energy; it's like riding on a roller-coaster.

Once your sugar levels shoot *very*, *very* high, the amount of insulin created is also *very* high. Now this is an extreme situation. It's like a road that gets totally jammed with cars (cars=glucose floating in the blood). When that happens, the body sends its traffic policemen (insulin) over there immediately to handle the situation. And because there are too many policemen all at once, they handle the situation very quickly, and send all these cars somewhere else pretty fast.

This seems to be a good thing at first, as the situation is under control, but suddenly you realize while this road is empty (the bloodstream) all the other roads have lots of traffic (which means lots of the glucose was stored as fat). Now when I say the main road is empty, I mean that there is now very little glucose in the blood which means the sugar levels have dropped, right? This again may seem to be positive as this is what the body tried to do in the first place, but because this was an extreme situation (and *too much* insulin was created), the result is also extreme. Now the blood sugar is *too* low!

Having your blood sugar level drop too low is not good either. When that happens, you suddenly feel drained of energy. And this is when you start craving sweets. Always remember cravings are a signal. It's your body calling out for an immediate blood sugar rise and nothing but sugary foods will cause it to rise quickly. So this is a vicious cycle.

The more processed the food = the higher the blood sugar levels = the more the insulin = the more the fat.

Not-so-good carbs

White sugar, sugar-containing products, all refined products such as white bread (chapatti, naan, parantha made with maida), white rice, white pasta, rice noodles, rice crackers, foods like cookies, sweets, cakes, carbonated soft drinks, condiments, ice cream and syrups

Good carbs

Whole grains (whole wheat, barley, couscous, quinoa, millet), wholegrain bread, wholegrain rice (brown rice, basmati rice, long grain), potatoes, raw vegetables, raw fruit

Good carbs versus not-so-good carbs When eating good carbs you can even eat a larger portion and your blood sugar won't rise as much as if you ate a small portion of bad carbs such as a white bread sandwich or a couple of cookies. So if you replace bad carbs with good ones, you can even eat a bit more and you won't put on weight easily from it.

Some good carbs to incorporate into your diet are wholewheat flour, buckwheat flour, oat bran, soy, rye, cornmeal, amaranth and semolina.

Sugar—the very, very bad carb

The most unhealthy carbohydrate has to be white sugar. Most forms of sugar, be it honey, molasses, maple syrup, white sugar or fruit sugar, cause acidity and fermentation. Various microforms (such as bacteria, yeast, fungus, mould) just love to be surrounded by sugar, and they ferment it into alcohol and create an acidic environment in the body. Eating white sugar on a regular basis is very bad for your body. Let's go through some facts about what sugar does to your body:

- Sugar decreases vitality and weakens the body's immune response to invaders, therefore lowering your overall immunity
- Sugar makes your blood more acidic, which results in vulnerability to toxins, bacteria and viruses
- Sugar feeds bacteria like Candida and promotes yeast infections
- Sugar is addictive and, of course, it is an extremely common cause of obesity as it has a severe impact on blood sugar levels, insulin levels, digestive enzyme count and the pancreas

The worrying thing is that sugar is hidden in almost every commercial food product you buy. We all know it is in foods like soft drinks, salad dressings and ketchup, but there's loads of sugar hidden in foods that don't even taste sweet! So always check the labels.

How to read a food label for sugar

When reading food labels, watch out for sugars hidden under different names:

Corn syrup	Mannitol
Corn syrup solids	Maltodextrin
Dextrose	Molasses
Fructose (high-fructose corn syrup)	Maltose
	Maple syrup
Galactose	Polydextrose
Juice concentrates (apple juice concentrate for example)	Sorbitol
	Sucrose
	Turbinado sugar
Lactose	Xylitol

There are many different forms of sugar called different names, but most of them are not much better than white sugar. You might have believed that brown sugar, Demerara sugar and molasses, for example, are the 'healthy kind'. But in fact these are virtually the same as white sugar—the only difference is that the last process of whitening and polishing has not been done, or some of the molasses has been added back after refining and processing. Molasses is what makes the colour of these sugars darker, which makes us believe they are healthier. Often brown sugar is simply white sugar coloured brown!

Healthy sugar substitutes

Honey

Honey contains at least fifteen nutrients, whereas sugar has none. It helps the digestion thanks to the presence of enzymes and it has a low glycaemic value, which means it doesn't raise blood sugar levels as high as sugar does, because it enters the bloodstream slowly. When buying honey, make sure it is 100 per cent pure. Experiment with different flavours of honey, especially the ones imported from Australia, New Zealand and Europe or search for organic wild honey from small villages in India. I generally use a teaspoon of honey in my tea instead of a teaspoon of sugar.

Agave nectar

Agave nectar is a juice extracted naturally from the core of living agave cactus plants in Mexico. It is a great sugar substitute for people with diabetes and hyperglycaemia. Agave nectar can be used for pretty much any kind of cooking or in your tea and coffee as it hardly has any flavour, so you won't even know you haven't used regular sugar. A teaspoon of agave nectar is equal to a teaspoon of sugar.

Stevia

Stevia is a great low calorie sweetener and it's totally natural. Stevia extract is ten to fifteen times sweeter than sugar so all you need is a few drops of the extract or just a pinch. It's available as a liquid or a powder and it is even grown in India so it is very affordable. Stevia can be bought in health food shops. I have even seen it in a few stores in Mumbai. However that was Mumbai, so it might not be available in smaller towns.

Fructose

Fructose is the chief sugar found in fruit, and it has a much lower glycaemic index than sugar. The great thing about fructose is that it pretty much tastes the same as sugar and you can use it for cooking or baking just as you would use sugar and you won't be able to tell the difference. However, it is still a processed sugar and is often derived from corn rather than from fruit, which is highly refined. So check the label of the fructose you are buying. Use fructose only when you can't use honey or Stevia, as these are much healthier options.

Jaggery

Jaggery, sometimes referred to as 'gur', is unrefined sugar that is made from sugar cane juice by boiling it till it thickens into syrup. The finished product can have a consistency as soft as honey-butter or as solid as fudge and its colour varies from golden brown to dark brown. Jaggery contains large amounts of magnesium, potassium and iron and it is a much healthier option than sugar and easily available in India.

Sugar substitutes that are better avoided

At one point low-calorie sweeteners (aspartame, saccharine, Splenda, etc.) were believed to be a great low-calorie substitute for sugar, but we are only now getting to know how bad for us they actually are! When used regularly, they can cause many side effects such as nausea, diarrhoea, recurrent headaches, dizziness and even visual disturbances, to name just a few. I don't think you should *ever* use these! You'd better have the sugar—at least that was once a real plant, while these other chemical substances come from laboratories and only time will show how dangerous they actually are.

Are fitness bars good for you?

Fitness bars are convenient whenever you're on the run or travelling, but there are only a few brands that make truly healthy bars. Most of the commercial 'fitness' bars you find in the market (especially the ones available in India), are filled with various forms of sugar, artificial sweeteners, hydrogenated and saturated fats, artificial flavours, etc. Some of these bars contain the same vitamins and minerals found in fruits and vegetables, but they don't contain the phytochemicals, bioflavonoids, enzymes, natural fibre and balance of vitamins and minerals found in these foods that are essential for the body to absorb these vitamins and minerals. Therefore I really wouldn't recommend any of these bars as they are very synthetic (and they do taste like that as well).

An exception would be organic, raw bars. They are 100 per cent natural and contain a balance of whole foods that are cold-pressed together so no nutrients are destroyed in the process. They are rich in fibre, antioxidants, protein (from hemp seed or soy) and good unsaturated fats (in the form of nuts or seeds). They contain no added sugar, no wheat or dairy products or trans fats, and most of them are vegan as well. However, most of these bars are not available in India at the moment. You could order them over the Internet I various sites that sell organic raw foods and supplements (just Google raw food and you get plenty of sites based in various countries) but it won't be cheap.

Protein

Protein is one of the basic building blocks of the human body, making up about 16 per cent of our total body weight. Muscle, hair, skin and connective tissue are mainly made up of protein. All proteins are made up of different combinations of amino acids. There are two types of amino acids: non-essential and essential. Non-essential amino acids can be made by the body while essential amino acids have to be received from food.

Animal proteins

Animal proteins such as meat, poultry, fish, eggs and dairy products contain all the essential amino acids. The healthiest option out of all of these is oily fish, as it contains healthy omega-3 and omega-6 fatty acids that provide protection against heart attacks and, to some extent, strokes. However, in terms of healthy eating, you should not rely only on animal proteins as many of them are high in saturated fat or cooked with a lot of fat (oil, lard, dripping). And I'm sure you are aware of all the bad publicity red and processed meat get nowadays. So if you are a non-vegetarian, do choose to eat more fish and poultry rather than red meat, and also eat a variety of plant-based proteins, as these are low in fat and high in fibre, vitamins and minerals.

Plant proteins

Plant proteins are legumes (peas, green beans), cereals, beans, pulses, grains, nuts, seeds, soya products and vegetable protein foods such as Quorn or veggie mince. Plant proteins contain many amino acids, but no single source contains all of the essential amino acids. However, there is no need for you to get all the amino acids in one single meal, so as long as you eat a variety of plant proteins, you should be fine.

How much protein do you need?

Our protein needs depend on our ages, sizes and activity levels. The standard method used by nutritionists to estimate our minimum daily protein requirement is to multiply the body weight in kilograms by 0.8 or weight in pounds by 0.37. This is the number of grams of protein that should be the daily minimum. So, for example, if your weight is 150 lbs, you should eat 55 grams of protein per day.

However, you don't really need to count or measure your proteins, because protein not only gets created inside our body from amino acids but it also gets recycled. What I believe is more of an issue today is having excess protein, and not the lack of it.

Excess protein creates acidity in our body and overloads our organs as our body needs to find a way to get rid of it. Some research suggests that too much protein can increase the risk of developing heart disease, stroke, kidney stones and osteoporosis. And if you are a non-vegetarian and eat some type of animal protein at every single meal, chances are you easily eat up to 200 grams of protein per day, which may be up to four times more than your actual need. Now imagine what a strain it is for your body! Digesting any meat alone takes four hours minimum so the more meat you eat, the less energy you are left with for the day.

Should you substitute your food with nutrition shakes or protein powders?

Many nutrition books suggest that you need to use nutrition shakes, protein powders or other supplements, or else your diet will lack essential nutrients. Conveniently enough these same books offer the instant solution: their 'magical' products! Reading the label, most of us would feel satisfied as long as we don't find words such as 'sugar' or 'fat' written on it, but what about the artificial sugars and other chemically enhanced ingredients?

The package is designed in such way that we end up believing the product is highly nutritious. On top of it, the label often has 'natural' written on it. I wonder how you can consider something natural if it has gone through so much processing? Looking at the label, you'll also notice that the product will easily last for two years. Does that sound natural to you?

Living bodies need living food—that's common sense. Would you eat a two-year-old piece of meat or a two-year-old apple? And that goes for all highly processed products. How about canned foods? Have you ever noticed how long they last? When you open that can of metal, warm up the contents and eat them, do you think you're getting 'nutrition'?

According to some experts, these shakes can also help you to lose weight as well! Yes, of course they do. And that's generally because you drink them instead of snacking on the unhealthy foods you would eat otherwise. They also taste yummy, so we don't mind replacing real food with them— because it's more like a treat. However, is it a good idea to replace a *meal* with a *liquid*? Well, it's not the best. It's not a big deal really if you do it, but you should know that having real food is always better. Why? Because some of the calories present in the food are used for the digestion of the same food, which doesn't happen as much if the food is turned into liquid. See, a liquid meal doesn't really need the stomach to work hard, which means less calories/energy will be used in the digestion. This is called a thermic effect and I shall tell you more about this in the weight loss section.

Sometimes it's really convenient to fix something and take it on the go when we don't have time. I myself rely on shakes or smoothies at times, however I make sure I use high quality stuff that is 100 per cent natural, and most of the times also organic. Recently I discovered a fantastic protein powder that is made of sprouted brown rice. It's called the Sun Warrior protein and it is available online on the Sun Warrior website. The company is based in the US but they have distributors in various countries all over the world.

This protein is not processed with heat (which means no nutrients are destroyed in the processing), and it has no sugar or anything artificial. I mix a scoop of this with some banana and a few spoons of yoghurt and water, and have it whenever I have no time to prepare a meal. The sad thing is, I can't even recommend this fantastic shake to you as it is not available in India at the moment. But if you have the extra budget to spare you can always search for websites with organic products and order some of these shakes. As I said before, I will provide a list of websites at the end of the book.

Just make sure you always read the ingredients list of any product, and if you find any alien sounding words in there, don't trust it. The best is to get organic, cold processed (or raw) protein powders that use stevia as a sweetener and certain only a few other ingredients. It is costly though and just note, it is not *necessary*! You don't really need extra protein. These shakes should just serve as a meal replacement at times, when you have no other healthy options available.

On the sets of Rakht

Years ago, when I was just getting into weight training, I hired a trainer for a few months and he suggested that I have a certain protein shake twice a day as he believed (as most trainers at that time would) that protein supplementation was essential and I didn't know any better then. There weren't too many brands available in India at the time and he put me on one of the more popular ones.

God, I loved that shake. It was thick and creamy and I enjoyed drinking it more than eating a normal meal. My trainer was happy with me as I began to put on quite a bit of bulk. I definitely felt strong, maybe almost too big. I remember a few people telling me I looked a little big, but I took it as a compliment (even though now I am not sure it was supposed to be one) as my trainer kept reassuring me I was in great shape. The only side effect I noticed was feeling bloated, but I tend to feel that quite a bit in any case.

Around the same time I got a job in a movie called Rakht. This was going to be my second Bollywood item number (called *Oh what a babe*) so obviously I wanted to be in the best shape ever. I trained even harder before the shoot, often doing an extra half hour of cardio in the evening. On the day of the shoot I was muscular like never before. My make-up artist used a tan-coloured foundation on my body so it looked as if I had just returned from a two-week vacation in Goa and thanks to the bronze colour, my muscles showed up even more. I thought I was in great shape, but when I saw myself on the monitor after taking the first few shots I was shocked to see that I looked quite big—as if I had put on weight.

We shot for four days and everyone said the song looked great, but I had my doubts as I really thought I was looking fat. My face looked kind of swollen up I swear! Anyway, the shoot was done, so there was nothing I could do. On the last day of the shoot I ran out of my protein shakes and the next day I left Mumbai and went travelling for work so I didn't have the chance to go and buy any more. Two days later I got a call from the movie producer saying we needed to shoot one more day for the song and reshoot some bits because of a technical mishap.

A week later I was on location once again. I got ready in a make-up van and then went onto the set, where I bumped into the stylist Ruchi, who was right at the entrance. 'Woooow! You have lost soooo much weight!' she said after scanning me from head to toe. Yeah right, she just wants to butter my ass, I was thinking. I couldn't possibly have lost any weight, I have not been dieting or anything and it's been just a week since she saw me last.

I thanked her and started walking towards the director to say hello to him. On the way, I got a few compliments on how great I looked but I didn't pay much attention to them, as this was normal. I think the crew considers giving the actors or actresses compliments part of their daily job. It's almost as if they have it written down on their worksheet: 7.00 a.m. arrive on the set, 7.05 a.m. tell the actress how great she looks. And later in the day, in case the actress is getting tired, remind her how great she is looking today. I don't generally pay much attention to compliments but if someone tells me I have lost weight, oh, they will have my full attention right away.

When I met the director, he also looked at me surprised and said: 'Yaana, have you lost some weight? You really look like you have! You look . . . well . . . overall kind of smaller.'

'No I don't think so, do I look like I did?' I said, hoping he would insist.

'Yeah, I'm quite sure!'

I didn't believe it till I saw the first few shots on the monitor. I really looked much thinner. But then, when you do this work, you also learn how much the light and the make-up can make you look drastically different, so I wasn't sure it was 'me' in a way.

When the movie was finally released and the song was played on TV over and over, I finally understood that the protein shake had made me retain a crazy amount of water, so much so that I looked fat. If you look for the song on YouTube (*Oh what a babe*) you will see the difference yourself. There are shots of me on a red bed dancing, wearing something black, and you will see I look much heavier there than in the other shots when I'm dancing with Sanjay Dutt wearing a white dress. The close-ups of my face also show a major difference. On the red chair my face is round and puffy and I look as if I was three kilos heavier than in the other shots.

This experience really showed me what unnatural, artificial substances can do to us. And you will hardly ever notice the effects as the symptoms are generally not as extreme. It's like being on medication for years; you don't know what you are building up towards and what kind of side effects the medication could have.

Does eating extra amounts of protein increase strength and muscle mass?

The answer is no, it doesn't. What increases strength and builds muscle is the stimulation of muscle tissues, which means strength (resistance) training. Any extra protein you eat will either get broken down and disposed of as urine or it will be used as fuel; however, any excess protein that is not used up or eliminated will be stored as fat!

Fat

Fat has got a very bad name in the past few years, thanks to a popular belief that fat *makes you* fat. This is another diet myth, one that can be very dangerous actually, because if you eat less fat than your body requires, you will face some serious health problems in the long run. Plus, if you want to lose weight, eating the right type of fat is absolutely essential as it helps to speed up the process of burning fat. In fact strange as it sounds, without fat the body will NOT burn fat!

Fat is a vital nutrient our body needs for everyday functioning. As an energy source, it supplies essential fatty acids necessary for brain development, growth, healthy skin, nails and hair, vitamin-absorption and the regulation of various bodily functions. Fat helps to balance your mood and make your brain sharp—in fact, without fat, the brain wouldn't be able to function at all. Did you know that more than 60 per cent of the dry weight of the brain is actually made up of fat?

My experience with a low-fat diet

If you've ever been on a low-fat diet, you probably came to the same conclusion that I did, that however low-fat the food you eat, it doesn't make YOU low fat.

I was on a low-fat diet for several years. In fact, to be accurate, I was not on a low-fat diet, but a 'no-fat' diet. I was simply petrified of fat and if I could, I would squeeze the last drop of fat out of everything I ate. I even developed tricks like using a piece of bread to absorb the oil from the food when eating out!

During those years, my hair became really thin, and my nails became so frail that I could literally peel them off. At the same time my concentration became really poor, and it would take me a couple of months to finish reading a book, because my mind was continuously drifting away. I kept telling myself that perhaps I was just not in the 'right space', but I couldn't really understand how that's possible as I used to read so much as a child.

Then one day I came across an article about how our brains function mainly on fat, and that our concentration is directly affected by the amount of the essential fatty acids in our diet. And that's when it suddenly struck me! I changed my diet overnight, and started eating raw nuts and seeds, plenty of extra virgin olive oil and occasionally fish or fish oil capsules. And guess what, it made a big difference. Just a few years ago I felt like I was using only half my brain, now everything is back to normal again, and all thanks to fat, I'm smart again!

Why fat is good

Most of us are conditioned to think that fat is bad for you. This is not true—in fact, it's quite the opposite!

The benefits of good fat:

- Lowers blood cholesterol level
- Lowers the risk of heart disease
- Improves the condition of nails, hair and skin
- Improves concentration

- Helps depression
- Strengthens joints
- Increases physical strength
- Improves insulin function
- Increases fat burning

Fat helps you to eat less

Fat also helps to curb the appetite and assist in weight loss, as it triggers the release of a hormone called cholecystokinin in the intestines. When this hormone is activated, the brain gets the message to stop eating, helping you to eat less with much less effort. When I was on a low-fat diet, it was always hard for me to stop eating. I would always crave more food and I would always end up stuffing myself. Even when I only had large amounts of vegetables, and I didn't have to worry about putting on weight, I just didn't feel satisfied. This changed when I started having good fats with every meal. Now I eat smaller portions of food, and it's enough, and my cravings have reduced.

Fat helps to burn fat!

And guess what, it gets even better—fat actually helps to burn fat! In order to burn the fat in your body, you need to eat the right type of fat. If you go on a low-fat diet, the body will NOT burn fat, because it knows it's not getting any more, so it will try to hold on to whatever it has. So eating healthy fats actually helps fat burning.

So, in a nutshell, a small quantity of fat is a must in your diet. Now I'll explain the different kinds of fats: the 'good' fats and the 'not-so good' fats.

Good fats

Good fats—unsaturated fats—are primarily composed of unsaturated fatty acids (which can be either monounsaturated or polyunsaturated). Unsaturated fats are derived from plant sources such as vegetables, nuts and seeds; they are also found in fish. Good fats are present in avocados, nuts and seeds, olives and fish.

One of the healthiest types of fat ever: fish oil

Fish oil is one of the best fats you can have as it contains omega-3 fatty acids. It has many health benefits such as:

- Lowers blood pressure and boosts the immune system
- Inhibits the growth of cancerous tumours
- Reduces joint swelling
- Lowers the amount of cholesterol in the bloodstream
- Helps to improve the texture of your skin and hair
- Lowers cravings for sugary carbohydrates and helps weight loss
- Decreases depression and improves concentration and learning capacity

If you can't take the smell or taste of fish, I would highly recommend you supplement your diet with fish oil capsules. It's fantastic for your brain; you will notice your concentration improve big time, and your nails, skin and hair will improve too. Fish oil capsules are one of the few supplements I believe we all should take daily, unless you eat oily fish (like tuna, mackerel, salmon, trout and herring) at least three times a week.

There are different brands of fish oil capsules, but some of these are of better quality than others. The quality depends on the way the oil was extracted. How do you know which is the best quality? You can do a little test at home. Squeeze the oil from a few capsules into a glass and place it in the refrigerator for five hours. If the oil remains liquid after those hours, it is probably of pharmaceutical grade, which is what you're looking for. If the oil is frozen solid, then buy another brand next time and try again. It's important to get the best quality you can afford.

Not-so-good fats

Not-so-good fats—saturated fats—are found in meats such as pork, beef, lamb, ham and generally all processed meats (like sausages, bacon, salami, etc.), and processed products and sweets such as cakes, pastries, etc. The white fat marbling you can see in beef and pork is composed of saturated fat. Some vegetable products such as palm kernel oil and vegetable shortening are also high in saturates. The more saturated fat you consume, the more cholesterol your body will produce, because the liver uses saturated fats to manufacture cholesterol. Therefore, excessive intake of saturated fats can significantly raise the blood cholesterol level and lead to other health problems such as an increased risk of heart diseases and stroke.

Very, very bad fats

Trans fats or hydrogenated vegetable oils are a common (and dangerous) ingredient used in processed foods and fast food. Margarine, for example, is a hydrogenated oil, and is extremely unhealthy, even though it's promoted as a healthy substitute for butter! Please don't believe the TV ads! These fats are bad news for your arteries and you should try and avoid them whenever possible. Fast food companies love them because they help increase the shelf life of food, which is great for their profits—but not necessarily the best thing for you. Trans fatty acids raise blood cholesterol levels and are also associated with heart diseases. The simple rule is, the more solid the fat is, the worse it is for you.

The fats list

Sources of good fats

Avocados	Olives
Nuts (raw)	Fish
Seeds (raw)	

All unrefined (virgin) oils:

Olive oil*	Grape-seed oil
Fish oil	Borage
Flaxseed oil	Evening primrose
Hemp oil	Cocoa butter
Pumpkin oil	Coconut oil (if cold-pressed)

Sources of bad fats

Beef	Egg yolk
Veal	Whole milk
Pork	Cheese
Lamb	Cream
Ham	Deep fried foods

Oils that are mostly sold refined:

Sunflower oil	Butter
Coconut oil	Shortening
Palm kernel oil	Margarine

*Some of the olive oil sold can be also be refined (and not virgin), so please read the label. Just because it is olive oil doesn't mean it isn't processed!

In summary

So remember, fats that have not been processed at high temperatures, and are therefore still 'virgin' (or unprocessed) are good for you. You should have plenty of these in your diet every day at every meal. To make this simple, just remember that fats that are liquid at room temperature are good for you (those are the unsaturated ones, for example virgin oils such as olive oil), while those fats which are solid when you take them out of the refrigerator are known as saturated (such as butter or margarine) and those should be avoided.

How to read food labels

If a product label says 'all natural' this may not necessarily mean it is good for you. The food industry allows certain man-made ingredients to be classified as natural. There are actually 15,000 ingredients that don't have to be put on the label. Similarly, just because a product is sold in a health food store doesn't mean it's really healthy. Always read the labels! If something is sold in a can, bottle or box, it simply IS processed and therefore not the best for you.

- The general rule for reading food product labels is, if the list of ingredients is long, the product most probably contains a lot of chemical additives and you should avoid buying it.

- Ingredients are listed in descending order by weight. The main ingredient is listed first, followed by other ingredients used in lesser amounts.
- The nutrition information provided is for the serving size identified on the label but that may not be the serving size you eat, so take that into account.
- Food additives are added in almost all packaged foods. Even if you buy packaged foods from a health food store, always read the label.
- Look for a breakdown of types of fat. Whenever a label says hydrogenated or partially hydrogenated oil, know that these are trans fats. Trans fats scar the arteries, causing heart disease and arteriosclerosis. Make sure you avoid buying products containing them.
- Watch out for healthy-looking labels that are just a trick of the manufacturers, as they design their food packages so they look 'healthy' and deceive the public. Always, *always* read the labels!
- Don't be fooled by 'fat-free' or 'sugar-free' signs on the package. Such products usually contain lots of carbohydrates therefore they are not calorie-free!
- Avoid any products with artificial sweeteners such as aspartame, Nutrasweet or Splenda. These are chemical sweeteners and cause a lot of health issues.
- Look out for products that say things like: '100% natural', 'all natural ingredients', 'No preservatives added', 'No artificial ingredients', 'Natural fruit flavours' and 'With *real* fruit juice'.

Water

We are all aware how essential water is for life. Our bodies are made up of 50–78 per cent water, and our brains consist of around 75 per cent water. Interestingly, most life on Earth contains roughly the same percentage. An individual cell contains 65–80 per cent water, fruits and vegetables tend to average about the same amount, some more, some less. Even the earth's surface consists of about 70 per cent water.

Water is necessary for all cellular activity in the body, as well as all bodily functions, including enzymatic activity, glucose utilization, nutrient delivery and waste transport, to name just a few. We may be able to survive weeks without food, whereas survival beyond seven days without water is impossible.

Water also takes care of your internal hygiene. The same way you take good care of your external hygiene by taking a shower every day, water performs a cleaning function inside your body. Imagine not taking a shower for a few days, or imagine how unclean you would feel if you had only three glasses of water to wash your entire body with! You wouldn't feel very comfortable, would you? You should try and make sure that there is enough water *inside* your body, so that the body can take care of its internal cleanliness.

How much water should we drink?

If you don't drink enough water on a daily basis, all of the body's functions will be compromised. And you know what—most of us don't drink enough. Just having enough liquids is not the same thing as having enough water. Tea, coffee and soft drinks do not count as a source of your daily water intake! These drinks only make you more dehydrated. So not only is this a bad form of hydration, it is negative hydration.

Whenever you do drink any of these, make sure you drink an extra glass of water.

Most fitness books largely endorse those well-known eight glasses of water. However, should there be any 'one-size-fits-all' prescriptions? I believe eight glasses of water should be the basic minimum but then you should also take in consideration your activity levels, how much you sweat, the weather conditions you live in and so on. Your body composition also makes a difference. The higher the fat percentage of your body, the more water you are likely to require. And if you exercise, you should also drink an extra one litre of water during or after the workout or else you may easily get dehydrated. During weight loss, drinking extra amounts of water is essential, as water is used to metabolize excess fat.

Diet is another factor you should take into consideration. If you eat lots of highly processed foods, you will naturally require more water in comparison to someone whose diet contains more fruits and vegetables (which contain a lot of water). You may have noticed that when you eat foods like breads, pasta or pizza, you feel very thirsty and you need to sip on a drink to be able to swallow properly, right? So, you do need to drink more water at those times.

How can you check if you are drinking enough water? Your urine should be colourless or have only a slight yellow tint. The only time your urine should be slightly darker is in the morning right after you wake up.

Drink lots of water in the morning

Most of us hardly drink any water after waking up, and instead immediately start drinking tea or coffee, which is dehydrating and acidic. Just as you brush your teeth and wash your face in the morning, make sure you also wash yourself from inside by drinking at least two glasses of water upon waking up.

In the winter, or if you generally like a warm beverage in the morning, have a cup of warm water with juice from half a lemon and a spoon of honey. It's the best morning drink ever! Drinking warm water during the day also helps weight loss according to Ayurveda. And it is surely more gentle on the body than drinking cold drinks, which is a shock to the system. I also recommend drinking plenty of coconut water since it is surely the purest (cleanest) water you can ever get, and it is also 'alive' as it contains enzymes.

Dehydration causes water retention

We normally assume that it is an *excess* of water that causes water retention, and not the lack of it, but the opposite is true. When there is lack of water, sensing a threat to survival, our body starts to retain every drop. Water reserves are stored in extracellular spaces (outside the cells), and this shows up as swollen feet, hands and legs. Another common reason for water retention is eating too much salt. The more salt you eat, the more water your body will store in an effort to dilute it. So remember, if you suffer from water retention, it's your body telling you, you need to drink more water!

What kind of water is the best for you?

The *quantity* of water is not the only thing you should care about, but the quality of water as well. Where the water comes from and what it contains, should be concerns as well. Our ancestors would have laughed their guts out if someone had told them that one day people would pay big bucks to buy something as ordinary as water in a bottle. But today, this is the reality and who knows what's next? One day we might find ourselves buying fresh air in a can! :-)

Bottled water is expensive. Buying bottled water when I was growing up in the Czech Republic was unaffordable for my family. The government always made it a point to say that tap water in our country is absolutely safe and healthy for us and people just didn't bother to find out further. My mom was a bit more health conscious though, so she would force me and my sister to get on our bikes every Sunday and cycle for two hours to a spring in the nearby forest to get our water supply for the week. There we would fill several plastic bottles with the precious liquid and head back. The water was then put in a refrigerator and drunk plain, as everyone enjoyed the taste. We treated it as something special and even though we often felt too lazy to make the trip to the forest, when the water ran out, one of us would always make the sacrifice. I suppose I developed a certain respect and appreciation for pure, natural water from that time.

A few years later, when I first started earning my own money by modelling and I could afford what most other teenagers couldn't, I started to buy bottles of mineral water wherever I travelled for my assignments. I wouldn't touch tap water, even though I had no knowledge of how unhealthy it could potentially be. I just instinctively felt it wasn't really good. It just didn't taste like I believed water should taste. Like the water from the forest spring that felt kind of 'alive' while tap water felt kind of 'dead' to me. So this habit of drinking *only* mineral water stayed with me for years, till recently, in fact, when I realized I was a bit too anal about it.

Yes, 'anal' is the word. See, I have an inclination to be obsessive about many things I do in life. And I am (or at least I used to be) obsessed with everything connected to health. This mineral water thing was one of my 'trips'. At one point, I even had my manager making sure that I got a particular kind of mineral water wherever I travelled for whatever job, which would at times be difficult, especially in small towns in India, where mineral water is not available in stores (please note, *packaged* drinking water and *mineral* water are NOT the same thing).

I never really tried to stress my manager out about it, but knowing me so well, she knew how much I cared about this, so one day it even got to a point that (without me knowing about it) she managed to have a client carry bottles of mineral water for me in her bag on a flight! When I found out, I felt kind of embarrassed that someone had to take so much trouble just because I'm . . . crazy?

Even then it was only a few years later when I finally managed to relax about the whole thing. I can't really tell you how it happened (it's still a surprise to me!). I think it kind of happened as one of the results of a transition I have been going through. A process of general acceptance of things in my life and life in general.

So while we should certainly care about the water we drink, and make sure it is the healthiest and purest water we can get our hands on, we can only do as much as we can financially afford. And of course if you do have the option and you have the money, then great, go ahead and buy mineral water every day. See, mineral water will always be superior to any other kind, be it tap water or the so-called 'packaged drinking water' (also referred to as 'table' water). The difference first of all is in where the water comes from. Packaged drinking water could be sourced from pretty much anywhere (municipal sources, ground water etc.). All packaged drinking water has to be treated by certain chemicals such as chlorine in order to be safe.

In comparison, mineral water emerges from underground sources, which are hopefully in a clean area, where it has flowed over rocks and is therefore high in mineral content. Tap water in comparison is not that good as it is simply recycled water. Many people boil their tap water and think that takes care of everything. This does kill most forms of bacteria—if you do nothing else to your water, at the very least you must boil it properly—but it doesn't remove the other contaminants. However, this may be your only option so what you should do is to get a good quality home filtration system. Filtration systems can be quite expensive and there are many different kinds. Of course, the higher the quality, the higher the price, which can go as high as a few lakhs. The Japanese have in the past few years come up with various systems that are excellent, as these machines not only filter the water but can also alter its pH value.

The pH of water is important as the body thrives better on alkaline water. Our diet is often quite acidic (all non-veg foods and processed foods are of acidic nature) so when you drink alkaline water, it dilutes the acidity created in your body. However, not many of us can afford such an expensive machine.

There are a few inexpensive things you can do to make your water's pH more alkaline, such as adding pH drops or natural calcium powder into the water, but the easiest of them all (and always available) is lemon juice. It's kind of a paradox, because we think of lemon (or lime) as something acidic, as it tastes acidic but the fact is, lemon is very alkalizing in the body. So add a few drops (or more) of lime/lemon into the water you drink sometimes. It tastes better and fresher too.

The healthiest drink ever

My absolutely favourite thing to drink is coconut water. There is hardly anything healthier you could drink. Even in comparison to the best quality mineral water, coconut water provides something that no other kind of water has, which is life in the form of enzymes.

Coconut water contains many vitamins such vitamin C, vitamin B, selenium and riboflavin and important minerals such as potassium, sodium, calcium, magnesium, phosphorous, iron, copper, sulphur and chlorides.

Coconut water is known to help digestion, clear the urinary tract, kill intestinal worms and help in the treatment of kidney and urethral stones, just to name a few benefits.

It is also considered to be a great sports drink because it is naturally fat-free, low in cholesterol and high in potassium and minerals, which helps the body to recover from vigorous exercise. It also has the same level of electrolytic balance as our blood.

So, instead of drinking sports drinks to replenish your electrolyte levels after exercising, a much better option is to drink coconut water instead. Anyway, sports drinks are generally filled with sugars, artificial sweeteners, artificial flavours, colours and other chemicals. You do not want to drink unnatural and artificial things like that!

In summary

So my friends, let's summarize it all:
1. Eat small meals throughout the day (every two and a half to three hours)
2. Compose your meals to include a portion of carbohydrate, protein and fat
3. Eat *real* food; replace all the highly processed foods and food products with foods in their natural state (less processing the better)
4. Avoid white sugar and deep-fried foods as much as possible
5. Avoid any artificial sweeteners and products containing them (soft drinks, diet products)
6. Make eating into a joyful experience, take your time to eat (eat slowly), eat with awareness and mainly ENJOY!

What I eat

Let me give you an example of what I eat during the day.

Upon waking up I drink two glasses of warm water with some lemon in it. Then I have some green tea and usually munch on an apple, while I take a few supplements such as a probiotic and multivitamin. I exercise soon after, which is why I don't eat anything big right away; however, I do make sure I eat *something*. If I get delayed, as I often read in the morning and get carried away, and feel hungry before I exercise, I might have a bit of plain yoghurt (just a small cup) with some honey and half a teaspoon of hemp or flax oil. (I love the taste of yoghurt with hemp oil!) Alternatively I may eat another piece of apple or some other fruit and have a few almonds with it that I soaked the previous night.

Then I exercise, which generally takes me half an hour (if I do my bodyweight killer routine) or up to an hour (if I do my lazy routine that consists of cycling on my home-use bike, dancing, playing with the hula-hoop and some stretches).

After I'm done exercising I have breakfast (well, breakfast number two in a way) which is usually a bowl of porridge with a bit of Stevia or honey in it. I like it simple and plain like this but if I am travelling and staying in a hotel I might order brown bread toast and an egg-white omelette (made of two egg whites) and some steamed veggies. I often travel carrying a few things with me (brown rice, olive oil, almonds, greet tea, honey) so if they bring the omelette prepared as I asked them (with as minimum oil as possible), I will also have a few almonds to get the good fat. I soak a few almonds every night and then eat them the next day.

What's in my handbag

If you opened up my handbag and searched through it, you would think that I'm a drug addict. Not only would you find a few suspicious looking two-inch needles (these are part of my first-aid kit—I do acupuncture), but you'd also find a couple of white powders. These often get me into trouble at airport security, but I'm up to any adventure and so far no one has tried to hold me back, especially not after I offer to let them taste them! (One of the powders is actually pretty disgusting so I doubt they'd believe it can give you any kind of ecstatic feeling.)

You must wonder what these are, right? Well the disgusting one (and the more suspicious-looking one) is a calcium powder, a special type of natural calcium derived from deep ocean oyster shells, that I add in every bottle of water I drink, to make the pH more alkaline (this is one of Cuckoo's specials; he himself has used it every day for more than twenty years). The second one is stevia powder.

Something else I carry in my purse is green or herbal teabags. Sometimes I collect them from the hotels I'm staying at (if they have good ones) and then enjoy drinking a healthy cup of tea on flights or in airport lounges. Having these with me saves me from grabbing black tea or coffee. Another great substitute that allows to you enjoy the taste of coffee without intoxicating you is a caffeine-free coffee substitute—barley coffee. It has a great taste, but doesn't make you dehydrated or acidic like coffee would.

When I next get hungry (which will be about three hours later or less), I have some baked or grilled fish with brown rice and some salad. For my next meal I may either have the same thing (I really enjoy it and I'm a lazy cook—I just throw everything into the steamer) or if I'm travelling maybe I'll have some dal and rice and veggies. The thing is, what I generally do is split the meal into two portions and have the second portion as my next meal. So if I am at home, I will just steam vegetables (zucchini, broccoli, carrot, mushroom, baby corn), make the rice in a rice cooker and steam the fish. I love my steaming system. It takes no time and it's yummy.

I don't even use any spices really, I just sprinkle some soya sauce on the food or use sea salt. I just love it this way. In the past when I had a maid who cooked, I would ask her to prepare yellow dal and palak, or some other sabzi and rice and I would have that, often combining it with the steamed fish or a bit of lamb.

If I am out, I may also have stir fried vegetables with tofu. To be honest, when I love something I can just keep eating the same thing every day, just like a dog does. I can easily have apples at least thrice in a day; they are my obsession. I would give up any food for the apple. I also really love brown rice, fish and dals. So I just keep alternating between all these.

It may look like I don't get enough variety and I don't really mind as I enjoy what I eat, but of course, for nutritional benefits, you should try to eat various foods, right? Well I end up doing that too because when I travel, it happens naturally. In hotels I often end up having a buffet lunch so I'll eat different things, or if I eat on the flight I also get different food every time. (I do try to avoid eating on flights; for short flights I can easily carry my own food from home or from the hotel but on long flights, I do eat the inflight food of course.)

I also eat the local food of the places I travel to. For example if I am in the south of India, I'll make sure I eat masala dosa or idli with extra coconut chutney (I could just live on coconut). If I am in Taiwan, I will eat the hot pot veggie preparation and all their tofu dishes. If I am in Goa at Cuckoo's I'll have the miso soups and sashimi made from the fish Cuckoo catches himself. If I am in the Czech Republic I will have my beloved duck. If I am in London, where everything is available and I can go to my favourite organic shops, I'll go and pick up this soy yoghurt I am currently crazy about, have some fresh-squeezed vegetable juice or wheatgrass juice

You do need to exercise if you want to be healthy—there is simply no way around it. Of course, if you lived on a farm and worked in the fields every day, are used to breathing fresh air and eating natural food grown by you and your neighbours, you might not need to exercise. But you probably don't live on a farm or work in fields, right? You probably live in a city; you have a sedentary job; you take a train or a car to work, hardly ever walking for more than five minutes at a time and then next to traffic, inhaling the pollution. You probably spend most of the day in an air-conditioned room, sleeping at night with the windows closed and the air conditioner on.

I sometimes wonder what kind of life we have made for ourselves. It is so artificial, so far from nature. How can we live like this and remain sane? Surrounded by cement, doing most of our activities indoors, with artificial lighting, artificial air, artificial food? Our bodies collect lots of garbage. And this garbage keeps growing day by day. Exercise is one of the few things that can help us get rid of some of this garbage and its toxins. Since the garbage piles up very quickly, the more often you take it out, the better it is. Sweating is the fastest way of getting rid of toxins, which is why regular exercise is so healthy.

So let's focus on how daily exercise can maintain and improve your health and what it actually does to your body from the inside.

When I first started exercising, I would only do cardio as my aim was weight loss and I never really knew that building muscle mass would actually help me to lose weight as well, also making my body look better, stronger and more attractive. Weight training (or any other resistance training) shapes your body, so instead of looking skinny like a stick, I would at least look like a woman. Nowadays, I don't even like the skinny look on women. I appreciate female curves, so I'd rather look at a female who has the curves and some fat than look at a woman who doesn't even look like a woman because she is too skinny.

I got into shape only when I started weight training—being skinny to me today doesn't mean I am 'fit'. There is a huge difference. While you don't need to train with weights to get fit and toned, you need some resistance. You could be doing yoga for example, because there you use your body weight, and you would build muscles. Any exercise that provides resistance will build your muscle mass and sculpt your body beautifully.

As I mentioned earlier I used to do a hell of a lot of cardio. I'd get into the gym and go from one cardio machine to another, spending ten or twenty minutes on each. I'd generally do the stepper or cycle for twenty minutes as I enjoyed it, while rowing I would do only for ten as I got bored quickly. I have a love-hate relationship with the treadmill—it's quite strange. There are times when I just love it and run on it every other day for six months in a row, and then suddenly I will stop and won't feel like getting on it for a year. It's also about how motivated or lazy I feel. If I get really high on coffee (which I try not to do anymore) I will get on the treadmill for sure and run fast, because it gives me a mental high too. But if I'm in a calm mood, I'd rather use the elliptical machine instead. Nowadays I love running outdoors, especially on the beach (not in Mumbai, but when I travel abroad or in Goa), but I can't get myself onto a treadmill in the gym at all. Also if I don't have good shoes with me (meaning proper sneakers) I'd rather do something other than run; good shoes are important because they give you soft cushioning so your joints are protected and the running is more enjoyable too.

How exercise helps to get rid of toxins

Exercise helps to clean all of your internal organs at the same time. As you exercise, blood circulates throughout the body and helps to bring nutrients to all the organs and muscles. At the same time it also helps lymph fluids circulate in the body, removing toxins and other harmful materials. When exercising you breathe deeply and therefore take in more oxygen, which stimulates all the cells and again helps them to remove toxins. You wouldn't want your poor cells drowning in metabolic waste, would you? That is what can happen without good circulation.

Of course, exercise triggers weight loss. Now fat is not just irritating, unaesthetic baggage that we don't want to carry around; fat is actually dangerous—it comes with the risk of clogged arteries, increased blood pressure and additional strain on the heart. Fat is also a good hiding place for toxins. In that context fat actually protects you, as the body wraps up toxins in fat so they don't float around freely in the body and cause harm.

Whatever exercise you choose, as long as you move, sweat and breathe, you are helping your body to get rid of toxins. It is up to you what form of exercise you choose; some prefer running, swimming, playing tennis; some prefer more indoor activities such as resistance training, yoga or Pilates. All exercise is good for you, and the more you love it, the more beneficial it is. There's no point in forcing yourself into doing something that you hate; it will only create negative energy in you, which will be unhealthy!

Exercise should become part of your routine, the same as cleaning your teeth or showering. It's a way of making your insides work more efficiently. And, of course, it will also make you feel more positive and give you more energy for the day.

Excuses

The most common excuse we give to avoid exercising is that we don't have enough time. I understand that some of us are busier than others, especially those with families. But, come on, let's be honest: is it really that impossible to find half an hour a day for yourself? Have you *really* tried? Because you know, once there is a will, there is a way, right?

I understand it can be difficult. I myself am not a parent yet, but whenever I do become one, I want to be able to give my children my best, which also means being physically fit enough to play with them. Besides, don't we all want to be a good example to our kids? Someone they want to grow up to be like? I'm sure you would like them to be strong, mentally and physically, right? You would want them to be confident and successful, wouldn't you? But can they learn all this by following *you*?

I am sure that if you tell your family that you are trying to find half an hour a day for yourself to exercise, they will support you. Maybe they will even join you! Half an hour is enough and it's a great investment, not only for your health but for your soul. The high you get after exercising is almost better than anything else. And when you feel good inside, it will affect those around you as well.

I know this half an hour is never just half an hour if you live in the city and you go to work out in a gym, right? By the time you get out of your house, get to the gym, change your clothes in the locker area, say hello to everyone, that half an hour is long gone and you have not even started working out. So we are not talking about half an hour really, are we? And many of us can't just go to a park and jog because there might not be any park close by. In Mumbai, there rarely is.

I wouldn't want to be jogging on the road between the cars really—I doubt it makes sense exercising to get healthier while you inhale all the pollutants!

However, you can easily exercise at home or even around your building. Any activity counts. How about taking the stairs instead of the lift? You can make it a rule. I always take the stairs and I love it as I know I'm working on my butt. When you really want to exercise, you can always find a way. I can't tell you how many times I have ended up running up the hotel staircases because their gym was either bad, or under renovation or not there at all. I never give up. I might run up and down the stairs for fifteen minutes and then go to my room, place a towel on the floor and do some crunches and push-ups. I sometimes go into the corridor and do lunges all the way from one and to the other. But be warned, you will get funny looks doing this!

So you see, there is no excuse that is good enough. You can always do it—if you want to. And if you don't, then just say you are not up to it. It's fine too; we are all lazy sometimes! I definitely am! But it's always better to just tell the truth, instead of making up excuses. It's a good practice. Why make excuses? For whom? For yourself? It's better to face the facts, accept them, because then a new window opens up. It's like standing at a crossroads. You keep saying you want to go left, but in fact you are not really sure. You know you 'should' but you don't actually want to, so you just end up standing on the spot. Nothing comes out of it. You will only feel bad for not taking a step. But if you say, 'Hey I really don't want to go left. I just don't,' then it's clear what you don't want, and this gives you new options. You can go right also, can't you? So if you are not up to exercising, then I'd say just admit it and then look for another option that would help you to detox and make you healthier (like the sauna or detox therapy). However, exercise has many benefits, and you can't really substitute all of them very well. And definitely not all at once.

So, even if you think that you are just not the 'type', and you simply don't want to exercise, give me a little chance over here to try to persuade you a little. Okay? Maybe motivation is all you have been lacking. What say?

Start today

Many of you have almost certainly tried some kind of exercise before, either joined a class or become a member of a gym, or at least gone running around the block in the morning several times. Some of us manage to make exercising part of our daily routine but, my guess is, the majority of us, at some point, get a bit lazy or uninspired and struggle to keep it going as the enthusiasm wears off.

That's generally because, unless you keep changing your workout routine and keep it new and exciting, at some point you get a bit bored with it. Of course, not seeing quick results is usually what makes us slow down or stop altogether. Whatever exercise you do will surely make some difference to your body shape, but unless the difference is drastic, at some point you may feel it's not worth the sweat, isn't it?

The basic problem is lack of knowledge about *how* to exercise, because if you knew exactly what you needed to do to achieve dramatic improvements in your body shape and fitness level at all times, you would surely feel inspired to exercise. Am I right? So let's get to it and fix this little problem. I promise you, *all* the basics you need to know to get into shape are *right here* in this book. I swear by it as this is all the information *I* needed to know to get myself in shape.

Aerobic and anaerobic exercise

There are two types of exercise: aerobic and anaerobic. Aerobic basically means 'with oxygen', while anaerobic means 'without oxygen'.

By aerobic exercise I don't mean the female tribe jumping up and down in leotards and sweating it out for an hour without stopping. Aerobic exercise is basically any activity in which oxygen is used. It is the most effective way of burning fat, because oxygen is needed to burn fat. Aerobic exercise is also called cardiovascular exercise, and from here on I will simply refer to it as cardio.

'Anaerobic' simply means without oxygen. It is also sometimes called resistance training, or weight training. Now, as I just told you that cardio is the most effective way to burn fat, you're probably wondering why you should waste your time doing exercise that doesn't burn as much fat. Why shouldn't you just keep doing cardio every day? Because that's pretty much like putting money in the bank in the morning, just to withdraw it again at the end of the day. The next day you are as poor as you were yesterday. No savings, no future. It's as simple as that.

With cardio, yes, you will burn the calories you just consumed, and then you'll burn some fat as well, but you won't really be any better off tomorrow. You will still need to burn the same amount of calories as yesterday, and you will need to eat exactly the same amount of food, because if you consume more calories than you burn during the day (including exercise), your body will store it as fat.

When you burn more calories than you consume in a day, you lose fat. When you consume more calories than you burn, you gain fat. With cardio it's as simple as that. Calories go in and go out, the same way money goes into savings and gets spent at the end of the day. So what do you do? How do you 'create' the savings so you're better off tomorrow?

$$Calorie\ intake < calorie\ burn = fat\ gain$$
$$Calorie\ intake > calorie\ burn = fat\ loss$$

The answer is: by speeding up your metabolism. And how do you do that? By building your muscles. The more muscle tissue you have, the more calories your body burns.

I can already hear the women saying that they don't want to 'bulk up'. Don't worry, that's not going to happen! I agree, when women get large muscles, like the women who do fitness competitions, they look rather unattractive. But do you know how these women start looking like that? With the help of steroids, hormones and other chemical supplements. Unless a woman uses these unnatural substances, it is almost impossible to get bulky or muscular like that, because the female body is naturally lower in testosterone (the muscle-building hormone). So, no, women really don't have to worry about becoming 'too big'.

Becoming 'too big' is the usual worry and the basic misconception about weight training. What you may not know is that fat actually takes up five times as much space as muscle! That means that if you gain muscle mass, which helps you lose fat in the process, you will not get bigger or bulkier, but smaller and leaner. Do I look big and bulky? I've been working out with weights for more than five years. And remember, it is always you who are in control of how much muscle you want to develop. It doesn't happen overnight. It's not like you wake up one day and realize you look like Arnold Schwarzenegger! It's your body and you can shape it as a piece of art, the way you want to.

So if you are doing endless cardio, yes, you will lose weight. And if you're happy looking like a small pear instead of a big pear, then that's totally cool. Do cardio and you can stop reading this book right here. But let me tell you, building muscles is very rewarding. You have no clue how superb you can look if you approach fitness in the right way!

By building muscle, you can make changes to your overall body shape. Of course, we all have a different body structure. But if you look at each one of us individually, you can work on certain areas, decrease them or increase them, and by doing this you can visually bring your body into balance.

Let's say you're not overweight, but your frame is quite big and your waistline is kind of thick, which makes you look shapeless. What you need to do in this case is build up your shoulders and butt, because as these become a bit bigger, visually the curve of your waist will get enhanced. That's just one example. You know your body better than anyone else. You know what areas you'd like to enhance and what areas you're not so proud of. So you can adjust your training accordingly and emphasize working harder on those particular areas that you want to enhance or conceal. It's the same principle as styling. If you've got great legs, enhance them by wearing a short skirt and who will bother to notice your 'bigger' belly?

This is just an extra bonus of resistance training. The main benefit is that it speeds up your metabolism. Now what does that really mean? It means that you will be burning more calories a day just by 'existing'. Just by living, surviving, staying alive. In other words, your Basal Metabolic Rate (BMR) will be higher. The Basal Metabolic Rate is the amount of energy (calories) that the body burns for regular bodily functions such as breathing, thinking, circulation, digestion, absorption, respiration and so on. It's the amount of energy you would burn at rest, lying down on a couch the whole day, without moving a finger. Now how does your body start burning more calories while you're resting? How do you speed up your metabolism? By increasing your muscle mass. The more muscle mass you have, the more energy your body needs to use in order to maintain it.

Let me give you an example. Imagine two friends sitting in a café. One is an accountant and the other is a secretary. They both work at the same office, spend the whole day sitting behind a desk with not much physical activity. The only difference in their lifestyles is that while the accountant runs every day or does some cardio activity, the secretary does resistance training (let's say she goes to the gym three times a week and does weight training or works out with kettle bells—a new popular workout tool).

After lunch both these women indulge in chocolate fudge and eat the same portion. Afterwards they return to their desks and work for the rest of the day. Now, if they have this chocolate treat regularly, who do you think is more likely to put on weight faster? Definitely not the secretary! Even though they both spent the remaining few hours at work sitting at rest in the office, the secretary's body burnt calories much faster than the accountant's body. Why? Because she has more muscles, and the more muscle you develop, the more calories your body burns to maintain the muscle.

There is no disputing the fact that the more muscle tissue you have, the more calories you burn at rest. And why does the body start burning more calories when you increase your muscle mass? Because your body needs hardly any energy to maintain fat, while much more energy is required to maintain muscle. You can see why it is absolutely essential to do not just cardio but some form of resistance training as well.

The best way to approach exercise is to alternate between cardio and resistance training. For example, if you do cardio on Monday, do resistance training on Tuesday, followed by cardio on Wednesday and so on. Of course, that's only if you manage to exercise every day, which I would highly recommend, especially if you want to lose weight. Rest is also essential, so if you do work out every day in a week, the seventh day you should not.

Some people prefer to do cardio and resistance training on the same day, but that's generally not the best idea. Why? Because if you do cardio before weight training, you will likely get exhausted and your strength will get compromised. The other way, if you do weight training first and then squeeze in cardio, your muscles will be tired by the time you start the cardio, so you won't be able to keep the intensity up. However, if you're done with your weight training and still feel energetic (just check if you've honestly trained hard enough), you can do an extra ten, fifteen, minutes of low-intensity cardio to burn some extra calories, if you want to. But again, don't overdo it.

Cardio

There are lots of things you need to think about to get the best cardio workout possible.

What is the best cardiovascular exercise?

There is no 'best' cardio exercise. Any type of cardio that gets your whole body moving, sweating and breathing heavily will benefit you. It is up to you to choose what you enjoy doing.

You should choose cardio that is tough for you, but not so tough that you can't manage to do it for more than five minutes. It needs to make you 'work out' and not 'hang out' while you read a magazine. I can tell you that if you're actually managing to read while you exercise, then you're not doing it properly. You should sweat so much that they have to come and clean the floor behind you!

It's rare to see people in gyms work out really, *really* hard—if you yourself work out like that, you'll soon notice the whole gym is looking at you, thinking that you must be preparing for a marathon or something! I have had people asking me questions like 'Are you a professional athlete?' or 'What competition are you training for?'. But let me tell you, it feels damn good when someone tells you such a thing. In fact, I consider these to be the best compliments I have ever received. To know that you can work out harder than most other people (including men) is really something that will make you feel proud of yourself. It feels like you can achieve anything in the world if you decide to, and nothing can stop you. Yeah!

So, what is the best cardio you can do? Let me just say it's not about *what* you do, but *how* you do it!

How to do cardio for maximum fat burn

As I hinted earlier on, the most effective way to burn fat is by doing a high intensity workout. Whatever exercise you choose, be it cardio or resistance training, the more intensely you do it, the more fat you burn. The good news is that you won't be burning the fat only *while* you exercise, but for the rest of the day as well.

Now how do you know your workout is intense enough? Whatever exercise it is you are doing, if you're working out as intensely as you should, you won't be able to do it for more than twenty or maximum thirty minutes. And you'll be dead by the end of it. In fact, I recommend training for just twenty minutes a day, but totally killing it.

If you exercise intensely enough in those twenty minutes, you will burn as many calories as you would in an hour-long 'take it easy' session. The difference is the after-burn effect that you get after intense workouts like that. Now, to be able to carry on with an intense workout for even twenty minutes, you need to learn how to train in intervals.

Interval training

Interval training means alternating short, fast bursts of intense exercise with slow, lower intensity ones. In practical terms this means that you work out as hard as you can for a few minutes, and then catch your breath at a lower intensity for another few minutes. When you work out like this your heart rate keeps going up and down and you burn a lot more calories in a shorter period of time.

As a solution for targeting maximum calorie burn, interval training is the best option, because it helps you to exercise for longer. I recommend you *always* do your cardio training in intervals. When you do high intensity, you should be well out of breath but not collapsing. Then reduce the intensity to catch your breath and start all over again. You'll begin to understand as you do it, and will get a better idea of how much intensity you can take and for how long.

One of the most recommended training formats is to choose three intensity levels such as low, moderate and high intensity. It's usually recommended to stay at every level for one minute, but you can also play with it and switch between just two levels—high and low intensity. (You can also do intervals as short as fifteen seconds.) It's up to you how you like to do it; as long as you work out as hard as possible, that's all you need.

Three-level interval training

Low intensity should feel easy, and is the period when you catch your breath. It could be a fast walk or slow run, depending on your fitness level.

Moderate intensity is reasonably tough. It should be difficult, but you should not feel completely out of breath. If you are running, it could be a fast run that you can maintain.

High intensity is where your workout reaches maximum intensity. This should be your peak during an exercise session. It should be the most intense level of exercise that you can manage to do for no longer than one or two minutes at a time.

Start with low intensity and switch levels after a minute each. But don't forget to warm up beforehand for at least five minutes.

For example:

1st minute—low intensity
2nd minute—moderate intensity
3rd minute—high intensity
4th minute—low
5th minute—moderate
6th minute—high
7th minute—low again
And so on . . .

There are many ways to do interval training. It's all about getting your heart rate up and down, that's all.

For me, interval training is also a good mental trial. You have to be totally present in the moment and watch what you're doing, because every minute you are changing the intensity of your workout. (This is usually done simply by adjusting the intensity level of the machine you're on, unless you are exercising outdoors or doing resistance training.) It's easy to get lost in thought while doing repetitive exercise—everyone does it. Interval training doesn't allow you to do that. You have to be mentally alert, and it is only when you're totally 'there' that you can push yourself hard enough and have a great workout.

It is also possible to use the interval training method while doing resistance training (body-weight exercises or using weights). All you need to do is not to rest much between sets and alternate between different muscle groups. For example, do one exercise for lower body (such as squats) and follow it by an exercise for upper body (such as push ups). This way your leg muscles get time to rest while you exercise your chest and you will build muscle but burn more calories at the same time. Another way is to alternate between short periods of rest and very high intensity exercise, for example do twenty seconds of jumping jacks and then rest for ten seconds and repeat the cycle four to five times and then switch to another exercise. I often do such a workout when I exercise at home. I use a timer that I set up for intervals so it keeps beeping, giving me a signal to start or stop exercising. I keep varying my routines, changing the interval times for exercise and resting and sometimes using only four or five exercises per routine and repeating them.

Types of cardio exercises

Running is one of the best calorie burners, but not suitable for everyone. If you're very overweight, have joint problems or are pregnant, you might choose cross-training instead. And don't forget to use good running shoes! Saving money and using shoes that are not made for running will only lead to injuries.

Walking is good if you're a beginner or overweight, but the fat-burning potential of walking is low unless you walk very quickly or on an incline (or up a hill). Check your heart rate to see if you're working hard enough (when using a cardio machine or by using a heart rate monitor) but I'd say that if you're not sure if you're working hard enough, then you're apparently not, because if you are, you will have no time to think thoughts such as 'Oh, I wonder, am I burning enough calories?' You will be busy trying to catch your breath and all you will be thinking is probably 'Oh God, fifteen seconds more . . . oh God, oh God.'

The elliptical machine is great for a fat-burning workout while developing muscle at the same time. It also reduces the risk of injuries since it removes the stress on the knees. You can also vary your body angle and therefore target muscles you want to concentrate on.

Cycling is great for interval training if you're on a gym cycle. Outdoor cycling is rather recreational unless you make sure you maintain the resistance and speed and don't coast!

Rowing is the most complete exercise because it works all the major muscle groups in the body. Because the movement also involves stretching, your flexibility and joint mobility improves as well. People with lower-back problems should avoid rowing.

Stair climbing is a great fat burner and a great lower-body workout. I love the stair climber because it makes me work on my butt while I'm burning fat!

Skipping is superb for interval training. It can get your heart rate up easily and you can do it anywhere. I carry a skipping rope when I travel because I never know what cardio machines will be at the hotel's gym where I'll be staying. You can also purchase a skipping rope with added weight, but if you're a beginner, the simple skipping rope will do.

Swimming is a superb full-body workout and a great way to relax your mind too. I feel very peaceful after swimming. After you're done with swimming, I recommend that you spend a few minutes just floating. Nothing feels as relaxing!

Kickboxing is fun and so cool. You can learn how to protect yourself, and burn a hell of a lot of calories at the same time. And who doesn't want to feel like Lara Croft or the Karate Kid!

Resistance training

Building muscle mass happens by exercising against resistance. The most common form of resistance training is training with weights (dumb-bells or machines) or by using body weight, stretch bands, water or immovable objects. Whichever form of resistance training you choose to do, as long as you are straining your muscles, it will work. It's up to you if you want to work out at home and do more body-weight training or go to the gym and use the equipment. The gym has its own benefits as well, one of them being the professional help you can get there. So if you are just starting off, it's a good thing to join a gym. However, it is not mandatory and working out at home saves a lot of time, so that's another great advantage. I'd say it's nice to alternate between both. Go to the gym on the days you do cardio and can't exercise outdoors (especially if the weather is bad) or when you want to train with heavy weights, and work out at home on the days when you have just those twenty minutes in the morning before you head for work. Also use the advantage of the trainers in the gym and learn new exercises from them that you can later do at home without any equipment (body-weight training).

The benefits of resistance training

1. Resistance training helps to lose fat. When you gain muscle, your metabolism speeds up, and the faster your metabolism, the more calories you burn at rest.
2. Resistance training has an 'after-burn' effect, which means your metabolism stays elevated even after the workout, so you burn more calories throughout the day. Cardio burns more calories during your workout while weight training burns more calories after your workout.
3. Resistance training shapes your body. You can enhance your body's overall appearance so it looks more balanced, firmer and fit.
4. Resistance training builds strength and endurance. It increases your energy levels through the day and helps you tackle daily activities with ease.
5. Resistance training increases ligament strength and helps your bones become stronger and denser. As muscles naturally start decreasing in size and strength with age, many people experience lower-back pain and joint problems, which can be avoided if you incorporate a resistance (strength) training programme in your life.

How muscles grow

In order to increase your muscle mass, you need to slightly 'damage' the muscle fibre by straining it. Straining or exhausting the muscle means putting it through an activity that is more strenuous than what the muscle has been used to. As they say, what doesn't kill you makes you stronger—it's certainly true in this case.

When you put yourself through physical stress, your body responds by adapting itself (i.e. by making itself stronger), so that it is ready to handle the same stress again in the future if needed. For example, if you go on a backpacking trip, walk the whole day and carry a heavy rucksack, you'll be dead tired after a few hours. But a few days later, carrying the same rucksack, you'll be able to walk for much longer without getting so exhausted. That's because your body has adapted and made itself stronger.

Another important thing to understand is muscles actually don't grow during the training; they grow *after* the training is done—but only if you allow them to rest and rejuvenate.

What kind of resistance training you should do

I myself am used to training with weights more than doing any other form of resistance training. However, please note, weight training is not the only (or the best) way to increase your muscle mass. Body-weight training, for example, is very effective, and I would highly recommend it. So are forms of yoga or Pilates.

If you are weight training, there are countless ways of exercising each and every muscle. If you work out in the gym, ask a trainer to show you what exercises you can do or what machines are available for each muscle group. You can start by choosing one exercise per muscle group and stick to the same exercise for a few weeks, increasing the weight and number of repetitions.

Some of the exercises might be more difficult for you than others. Start with the simpler ones and as they becomes too easy or repetitive, use variations. But remember, intensity counts, so don't avoid the more difficult exercises just because you're lazy!

Resistance training—all your questions answered

Here are some of the basic questions about resistance training answered.

How important is warming up?

A warm-up is essential because, if you do strenuous exercise without a warm-up, lactic acid builds up in your muscles, which causes fatigue. Lactic acid is created when there is not enough oxygen being delivered to your muscles, which happens with sudden exertion. However when you do warm up, your heart and lungs gradually start delivering more oxygen to the muscles, so by the time you start exercising strenuously, there is plenty of oxygen circulating, which prevents the oxygen debt that causes the fatigue.

Can muscles turn into fat?

Fat cells and muscle cells are totally different types of cells, so there is no way one type could be magically transformed into the other. So when you see a big guy who, once upon a time, was very muscular and now he is rather fat, trust me, his muscle didn't turn into fat (as believed). What probably happened is that he stopped exercising, but kept the same diet and, because his calorie expenditure was much less, he obviously put on weight. Also, as you lose muscle, your metabolic rate decreases and you burn less calories.

Can you reshape muscles by isolation exercises?

No. You cannot reshape muscles, you can only make them bigger. You can however reshape your body by emphasizing certain muscle groups and exercising those harder (and making them bigger), which will then help to change the overall shape of a certain area of your body or all of it.

Getting the perfect abs

Did you know that you won't get a flat stomach by exercising your abs? If you have fat in your midsection, it won't disappear by doing crunches every day, but by burning the fat through cardio! Sorry to burst your bubble, but there is no such thing as a spot reduction. The fat on your belly will go at the same time your overall body fat percentage lowers. In fact, even if your abs are in a great shape you won't see them unless you get rid of the layer of fat above them. So don't try to exercise your abs every day, thinking that will make your stomach flat. Do more cardio instead.

Exercise and progress

In order to get the best results your workout always needs to be progressive. That is because your body easily adapts to any repetitive routine and if that happens, you will start stagnating. In other words, your body will reach a so called 'plateau'.

Let me give you an example of this from my own work background. As you know I work in the Bollywood industry and from time to time I shoot item songs for movies. These shoots are really exhausting because you end up dancing the whole day, but unlike the other female dancers I do still get time to rest in between the shots. Looking at how hard the other dancers worked, I often wondered why so many of them didn't seem fit enough. Their diet perhaps wasn't the best, but with all the physical activity they did, they could be having chocolate cake for lunch and they would surely still burn it off.

So how was it possible that some of them seemed overweight? The answer is simple. It's because they do this every day! See, their body is used to this routine. And this is why you need to make sure your work out is *always* progressive.

So whatever exercise you do, push yourself a bit harder every time. However, remember that the progress should be *steady* and *gradual*. Don't overdo it by trying to do all your exercises in just one session. If you do that, you may not be able to walk for two days or even sit on a toilet seat! Ouch! Plus you could also seriously injure yourself and then the fun is totally over. So be careful, okay?

Part of progress can also be making your lifestyle more active. For example, walk your neighbour's dog (if you don't have one), cycle to work instead of taking a bus, or get off the bus one stop further from your destination. Join dance classes in the evening, take the stairs instead of the lift and so on. I'm sure you can come up with more options. Everything counts!

The plateau

If you ever feel you have reached a plateau (i.e. your body has stopped showing results), you should ask yourself a few questions:

- Is your workout progressive enough?
- Have you been exercising as intensely as you can?
- Do you train regularly or do you skip workouts here and there?
- Is your diet as good as it should be?
- Have you been eating properly, five to six times a day?
- Have you been on time with your meals?
- Are you having healthy, small portions of food?
- Have you been getting enough rest?
- Are you sleeping enough?

- Have you been partying too much? (Alcohol is also concentrated carbs!)

By answering these questions honestly, you'll probably find the reason why your body started stagnating. However, if you feel you have been working out really hard and your diet has been excellent, there might be some surprising reasons for the plateau. You might be overtraining, or have insufficient calorie intake. Remember you need to rest and you need fuel to burn the fat!

I too have plateaued a few times, just because I didn't eat enough. Initially I couldn't understand why, because I was working out so hard! Then I went on a holiday, ate much more than usual and worried that I would put on weight. To my surprise the exact opposite happened! I looked much better after my holiday! That's when I realized that I had reached a plateau because I wasn't eating enough.

How to progress with cardio
- Increase the tempo or intensity
- Make it harder (by using elevation for example)
- Increase the length of the workout (increasing intensity is better for fat burn)
- Change the type of exercise to one that is more difficult for you

How to progress with resistance training
- Increase the number of repetitions
- Add an extra set (do one more set of the same exercise, or choose a different exercise for the same muscle group)
- Change the exercise to something more difficult
- Decrease the resting time in between sets
- Increase or decrease the amount of leverage (resistance). For example, instead of doing normal push ups, you can place your legs on a higher surface such as a stool,

which will make the exercise more difficult. When weight training, increase weight

- Do the exercise on an unstable platform, for example, do push ups while placing your hands on two balls, or do squats using a bosu ball. (The bosu ball is an exercise tool that looks like half a ball and wobbles from side to side when you stand on it. It's great for using your core strength while you exercises.)
- Do a cardio exercise, such as skipping, running, kicking, for one minute in between sets instead of resting

Weight loss

By now you should have realized that I don't want this book to be an ordinary diet/weight-loss book. But I guess some of you must want some tips from me about this. So here goes. However, if you do decide to go on a weight-loss mission, please do it as wisely as you can, giving your body enough nutrition at all times and not killing yourself in the gym. You can lose weight and keep it off by doing everything in a non-harmful way, just by following the good eating advice here and exercising. It will take time though, but remember the more gradual the weight loss is, the more permanent it will be.

How to lose weight

To lose weight you need to create a calorie deficit. There are only two ways to achieve this. One is by eating less calories than you burn and the other is by burning more calories than you eat. So what's the best way? When you eat less, you will lose weight (at the cost of nutrition and your sanity) but your metabolism slows down, and to keep the weight constant you will have to eat less and less for the rest of your life, which is of course unachievable. This is what happened to me. So evidently, the answer is the second option. Burn the fat! And stick to a sensible diet as much as possible according to the principles I set out earlier.

Weight loss versus fat loss

Weight loss and fat loss may be two different things. If you are losing weight, it doesn't necessarily mean that you are losing fat. Let me explain. See, if you weigh yourself every day on a weighing scale, you will notice that your weight often fluctuates. Most of us would link it to something we ate on a given day, which is why we feel guilty and promise ourselves not to eat that burger again. But the actual reason for your weight fluctuation is usually the water content of your body, which keeps changing as the day goes on, depending on many factors—such as what you ate or drank, your activity level during the day, the amount of sleep you had, the weather and so on. Our body consists of around 70 per cent water, and it is natural that this amount keeps fluctuating.

So if the weighing scale suddenly one day shows that you weigh half a kilo more, don't panic. It's probably just water retention. It's the same if your weight suddenly drops—the difference can be up to one kilo. There is no reason to celebrate as yet. You may still have the same amount of fat as before.

Another reason for sudden dramatic weight loss may be loss of muscle tissue. This is of course bad news. You can lose muscle due to insufficient calorie intake or if you stop exercising—muscle needs maintenance too. That, of course, doesn't happen overnight, but if you drop your calorie intake too low, it starts happening pretty quick.

What I am saying is that the weighing scale can't really tell you what it is you are losing: water, muscle or fat. Therefore it doesn't really make much sense to keep weighing yourself every day and anticipating the countdown. What you need to focus on is not weight loss, but fat loss, and fat loss cannot be measured with a weighing scale. You should also keep in mind that fat is quite light compared to muscle, which weighs much more. So if you do resistance training and shape your body, you're not going to notice much difference on the scale, in fact you may weigh *slightly* more, which will be a sign that your body is gaining muscle, which is heavier.

How much body fat should you have?

There is no such thing as having zero body fat. Fat is necessary for survival, so get your head around that. Having too low a body fat percentage is unhealthy and dangerous. Once again, balance is the key.

The usual recommended healthy norm of body fat percentage is between 8–19 per cent fat for males and 21–33 per cent for females. You can check your fat percentage regularly and compare it to these statistics but I myself don't really believe in that approach. These are just numbers. If you are not happy with the way you look, you just won't feel comfortable even if you technically fit the range.

So it's really up to you and what you want to look like. A good idea may also be to ask your partner about it, because there is a good chance that while *you* think you are fat, your partner actually thinks you are perfect and wouldn't want you skinnier at all!

The last time I checked my own fat percentage must have been about four years ago. I remember it was around 19 per cent but I definitely felt I needed to lose some fat at the time (the problem was I ALWAYS felt I needed to lose fat, whatever shape I was in). The thing is, you can keep checking your fat percentage every month—it may even motivate you, provided you are losing the fat. But what if it shows that you have not lost fat at all, or that you have even gained some, will you feel bad? Will you feel unhappy? Will it stress you? Or will it motivate you? It all depends. If you think it will only motivate you, then go ahead. But if you feel it may add extra pressure or make you feel guilty or disappointed, then I wouldn't recommend it. You should focus rather on how you feel inside your body (healthy? fit? strong?) and not how you look in a bikini.

Kingfisher calendar

You might have heard about the Kingfisher swimsuit calendar, right? Well in case you haven't (which would be a great sign as it means you are probably not a TV addict and you have better things to do than read page three of the papers), the Kingfisher swimsuit calendar is a very posh calendar and a dream project to be a part of for any Indian model. I was selected to be one of the models for the calendar for two consecutive years, which is quite a big thing as no other model has done it that many times.

I remember how stressed I would be before the calendar shoot every time, as I never thought I was in good enough shape. So I would exercise for two hours a day (in the morning and evening) and I would diet too. I would either do the low calorie diet, which would mean I'd just have some salad, vegetables and fruit, and coffee of course (oh tonnes of coffee in fact, as I needed to get a kick for the workout), or I would go on a low-carb diet.

I was really tense before every shoot. I even remember asking Atul Kasbekar (the photographer) if we could do my shots early in the morning instead of in the afternoon, because I knew that in the morning on an empty stomach my belly would be more flat. On the day of the shoot I always hoped that I would get a swimsuit to wear instead of a bikini, or some accessories that would cover me up a little. I don't think any outsider looking at the pictures can even imagine how uncomfortable the model may be! Some of us women don't even feel okay going swimming in a bikini; now imagine posing in it!

I also remember how I used to eat hardly anything all day, till we'd finish the shoot, as I was afraid I might bloat up, even though I think there was another reason for it too. I needed to 'think' or 'believe' that I was skinny and it's easier to think you're skinny when your stomach is empty and not when it's full.

Why am I proud of myself now?

Well recently, my manager told me I was asked to be part of the Kingfisher calendar once again this year.

I agreed to do the shoot but I wasn't very enthusiastic about it at all to be honest, because I immediately remembered what I used to go through before the shoot just to get in shape. I can't do it this time, I thought to myself. I just won't. I can't because I don't care anymore, and at the same time because I do care a lot. I care about my body and my mental state! And I am not willing to do anything unhealthy to my body. Those were my first thoughts, but at the same time I knew I would at least make sure I worked out every day and ate properly and healthily.

However, since the time I got to know about the shoot, I have been on the road a lot. I was travelling every few days and I have also been a bit unwell so, simply, I haven't spent a minute in a gym or lifted anything heavier than a bottle of water. Plus I have been eating bread as I told you! And I am loving it! I just had this most amazing sandwich at the airport. It had goat cheese in it, and when I ate it I was in heaven, enjoying every single bite and just loving the fact that I am no longer afraid of bread. Now imagine, I had two weeks to go till the calendar shoot. And when I thought about it, and ate bread at the same time, I wanted to laugh, even though there was nothing funny about the fact that I am in far from my best shape, and I was about to shoot a swimsuit calendar!

Ultimately the shoot didn't work out but I still feel joy because this is officially my own little personal victory. After all the tension I have gone through over the years and all the torture I have subjected my body to, I have finally decided to never ever led anything whatsoever put me in such a state of mind. And it's not an easy thing to do when you know your body will be ogled at by the whole nation, huh? And that's why this is a victory for me. I have finally grown into the woman I have always wanted to be.

How to measure fat

The best way to measure fat is with callipers (a simple measuring tool that looks like a ruler), which are inexpensive and easy to purchase. If your gym has a fitness-test machine that also measures the lean body mass, water content, metabolic rate and so on, there's nothing like it as it will give you a chance to monitor your progress and adjust your training according to your goals. You should do this test every three weeks. There are other ways of measuring fat, such as hydrostatic testing (in water), but they're not used much. There are also small home-use fat monitors, but these are often not very accurate, so don't waste your money.

The speed of weight loss

The speed of weight loss depends on many factors. First it is your body type and composition. We all have different metabolic rates, digestive capacities, hormonal profiles, blood groups, fingerprints, etc. That's why our bodies also respond differently and the speed of losing weight will differ from one to another. Some people lose weight faster than others or put on muscle very quickly, while others are less fortunate and they need a bit more time to get there. Some of us are also predisposed to have more fat cells than others, and women generally have more fat cells than men. However, we all can improve our physiques and fitness with the right effort.

How fast you lose weight also depends on your previous lifestyle. If you've been dieting a lot before, you might take a little extra time to lose the fat because your metabolism is probably slower than it should be (thanks to all the dieting). But don't worry. Eventually, as your lean body mass increases, your metabolism will speed up and you'll burn fat with ease.

I know we all want to lose weight as quickly as possible, but that's not actually the best way to go about it. When you start a weight-loss mission, the first week you may lose as much as one kilo, but that is mostly water, so when the speed of your weight loss (according to the weighing scale) naturally drops from the next week onwards, don't worry, you are not doing anything wrong! Also bear in mind that if you are losing more than half a kilo a week, you are most probably losing muscle mass, which is not good. So don't try to rush it!

For maximum fat burn, exercise on an empty stomach
Doing cardio first thing in the morning (on an empty stomach) is known to be the fastest way to burn fat. I'm not saying that you *have to* do cardio only in the morning as you will burn fat any time of the day you choose to exercise but, on an empty stomach, you will burn more fat than you would *after* you have eaten breakfast.

Let me explain why. When you exercise, you need energy. The first source of energy your body uses is carbohydrates (glucose) from the food you have just eaten. It is once the first source of energy is depleted that your body uses the stored energy (i.e. fat). In other words, it is only after you burn your carbohydrate reserves that you will burn fat.

When you wake up in the morning, you won't have eaten for about eight to twelve hours and the level of glucose stored in your body (glycogen) is very low. If you work out during that time, your body has no other option but to use fat as fuel. I used to do this whenever I wanted to burn as much fat as possible in a short period of time, like before a swimsuit shoot. It just burns off a little extra fat in comparison to working out later in the day after you have eaten. How much exactly would be hard to say as we have different bodies and burn fat at different rates, but it definitely burns an extra bit (and any extra bit is good if you have a deadline approaching right?)

Another benefit of early-morning cardio is that your insulin levels are low, because insulin is released only when you eat. That is good news again, because insulin interferes with the burning of body fat. If less insulin is released, more fat is burnt. However, on the day you do weight training, I recommend you eat before you work out. You'll need a lot of energy, or else your workout will get compromised. The best option is to eat an hour and a half before you start your workout so by the time you're done it's just about time for the next meal. However there are some for whom it may not be the best idea to work out on an empty stomach as their blood sugar can get so low that they feel weak or sick. Remember, we all have different body types, so you do need to follow your body! I had a friend who fainted after running to catch a bus early in the morning few times as she was late for work—all because she didn't eat breakfast!

What intensity of exercise is the best to burn fat?

According to research, lower-intensity cardio burns a higher percentage of calories *from fat*, while the higher intensity burns more calories *from the carbohydrates* you have eaten that day. Does that mean that lower intensity is better? Not really.

What counts at the end of the day is the total amount of calories burnt, and if you do low-intensity cardio, you won't burn that much. Higher-intensity cardio also increases your metabolic rate after the workout, which means you'll also burn more calories long after your workout is done. High intensity workouts are, as I have said before, the best option, but unfortunately are difficult to sustain for long periods of time. That's where interval training comes in handy!

Is spot reduction possible?

Fat is stored in almost every part of the body. A small amount of fat is stored in muscles (intramuscular fat) and the majority is stored around the organs and beneath the skin. How much and where you store the most fat depends on your genetic make-up and your hormone balance. Unfortunately there is not much you can do about the way your body distributes fat. But you can definitely control *how much* is being distributed! So, as I mentioned earlier, trying to work out a particular area of your body (such as your belly) harder, thinking it's going to melt the fat there, is not going to help.

When weight training, do more repetitions burn more fat?

No, they don't. The harder you work out, the higher your heart rate goes and the more calories you burn. So in that sense, it's better to do fewer repetitions with heavier weights, which will be more difficult for you to accomplish than doing endless repetitions with lighter weights. What burns the fat is the increased metabolic rate after weight training, which has nothing to do with the number of repetitions. The higher metabolic rate, caused by muscle growth, is what burns fat, and far greater muscle growth is achieved by doing less repetitions using heavier weights than by using lighter weights and doing more repetitions.

The low-carb diet

Okay, you might be saying it's all very well to gradually work towards fitness and health but what if you have a wedding to attend in a week's time and you really, really want to lose some weight really quickly? What advice would I give you then? I'd probably tell you to cut down on your carbs as much as you can—that would bring you the most drastic results. The thing is, once you know how well a low-carb diet can work (and it does work amazingly well for a short period of time), you will always prefer this diet to any other. However, it comes with a big BUT as you know. I don't encourage anyone to get on this diet unless there is a very strong reason for it (like your own wedding) as it's not a healthy thing to do. I wouldn't do it myself, meaning I wouldn't go on a diet for my own wedding (generally because I have gotten over the whole issue of 'looks') but I totally understand that most women out there consider this day to be the most important day of their life and they want to look their best. But do look at the section on carbs in this part of the book, where I talk about why low-carb diets are ultimately so harmful.

Some weight-loss tips

Additional things you can do to help weight loss

Any therapy or treatment that helps your body get rid of toxins will aid weight loss. Toxins are locked up in your fat cells so, as long as you have toxins within you, your body will try to hold on to the fat (fat cells) in order to protect you from these toxins, because they are safer inside the fat cells than floating around your body causing more damage.

Detox-aiding therapies include:

- sauna
- ozone therapy
- colon hydrotherapy
- liver and gall bladder cleanse
- heavy metal detoxification
- rebounding (jumping on a trampoline)
- praanayama (yoga breathing)
- herbs and teas that aid detox
- nutritional support for liver, kidneys (detox organs)

Create a support system around you

Surround yourself with friends who can support you on this journey, and avoid those who discourage you in any way. One great thing to do is to go on a weight-loss mission with a friend or a partner. But this generally works only if the other person is as excited and determined as you are; if not it could work against you. So be very selective and careful when choosing your weight-loss buddy. You need someone who can motivate you enough to get you out of bed on a lazy day, someone who is going to be there to push you when you are contemplating skipping a workout!

Monitor your progress

Take a picture of yourself when you start on the mission and then take another one every three weeks. The changes your body goes through will inspire you along the way and motivate you to keep going.

Create an exciting challenge for yourself

Sign up for a marathon or any other challenge. It's not about winning but participating! Don't worry if you think you'll make a fool of yourself. It's all about just *doing it* and proving to yourself that you *can*. It will give you strength and confidence. Another great idea is to make a bet with your friends on who's going to get into better shape faster or within a certain period of time. You can do the same in your office with your co-workers. Start a little competition! It will give you a goal to work towards and inspire you to work out harder. Plus it's fun!

Use the power of visualization and positive thinking

As they say, 'No person ever became successful by thinking about failure the whole day.' So make sure you stay positive and believe in yourself at all times.

It's also helpful if you note down your exact goals (with dates attached) and imagine how you'll feel when you achieve them. You can also cut out pictures from fitness or health magazines (your fitness idols) and stick them onto a sheet of paper or in your workout diary so you can look at them before your workouts or whenever you lack motivation.

Write some positive affirmations in your diary, such as things you would like to achieve (fit and healthy body, confidence, power and so on) and whenever you come across the things you have written, imagine how it will feel when you get there. It's best to make full sentences, such as 'I have the greatest body ever', 'I am super healthy', 'I am (whatever you wish to be)' and keep reading them often and 'feeling' as if they were already true. This will fill you with positive energy and help to attract what you desire. Believe me, it does work! It's called the 'law of attraction'. When you become clear about what exactly you want in your life and focus on it regularly, it's like instructing the universe to deliver.

Even if this sounds like a childish game, just give it a try. I have been using this method for years, to attract the things I want in my life, and I think you would agree it has been working for me quite well, isn't it? So figure out exactly what you want, and focus on it every day.

In conclusion

I have given you all my hard-earned knowledge about weight loss and fitness in this section. And I hope it helps you. But as I have said before, you can lose all the weight you want, but if you're like what I was, someone who is never satisfied with how you look, no diet in the world will make you feel good. So its time to move to the next section and work on what I call 'diets' for the mind.

Part 3

How to Love Yourself

Photographs by Prasad Naik

In the last section I taught you all my tricks to eating and exercising right but, as I told you in part one, it doesn't matter how good you look—if you don't love yourself you'll never feel really happy or satisfied with what you see in the mirror. Ultimately it's all about loving yourself. My friends ask me, 'So how do I start loving myself Yaana?' 'Well you just do it!' I am tempted to answer back but I know this won't do. So in this final section I have organized my thoughts into some practical tips which I hope can really help you. They have come from my own experiences, my reading and my chats with Cuckoo. Think of it as an A to Z of loving yourself.

It's everywhere

I'm sure all of us could write a long list of things we dislike about our bodies. The wrinkles, big feet, flat butt, small breasts, stretch marks—the list can go on and on. Remember the last time you went shopping? Would you be able to count how many times you ended up looking at your reflection in the store mirrors? Don't we all do that? Now what do we see? A great-looking woman or man, with a big smile on their face? Dream on, right? There is always something or the other to be fixed, isn't there?

To have negative body image is very common and 'normal', although certainly not natural. There is no way out of it. However much weight you lose or whatever body treatments or cosmetic surgeries you undergo, having negative body image has nothing to do with your actual body looking the way it does. Diets or surgeries can't fix it—it's all in your head and no doctor or surgeon can enter there. My story is the perfect example of this.

Now what if I told you that you are already perfect the way you are, right now. Would you believe me? Of course you wouldn't! You have been told that you are not good enough since childhood, so it's a bit hard to suddenly start believing otherwise. Your mom may have scolded you when you got bad grades and you ended up feeling not smart enough; your friends or colleagues used to advise you to lose weight or dress differently; the media has been bombarding you with manipulative messages making you feel negative about your body. The pressure is everywhere and it is so extreme that it almost makes us feel that being 'normal' and not looking like a model is some kind of a disease! So before we begin to learn to reprogramme our brains about our bodies, let's see if we can throw out some of the negative thinking in our lives. While some of what follows may seem unrelated to food and our body image, bear with me. Often our insecurities about our bodies arise from a deeper well of feeling low about ourselves. So let's start with this first and then I promise to spend lots of time talking about our bodies!

The glamour mirage

Guess what, most of what you see on TV or in fashion magazines is unreal anyway. It's an illusion. The models' images go through quite a bit of retouching, making them look like goddesses, while they are just normal people with flaws just like anyone else. I do this job so I know. My friend Bini, who is a professional make-up artist, often tells me stories of models coming to shoots with allergic reactions, swollen eyes or bruises and she manages to fix them all up with make-up tricks and layers of foundation and make them look as beautiful as ever. Then of course Photoshop's magic is applied, the tummies are tucked, cellulite airbrushed and, wow, the end result is fabulous—a perfect human is created. And if something goes really wrong it's even possible to put the model's head onto someone else's body! The impossible is possible today, so why not take advantage of it? I can tell you that even the models with their 'perfect' bodies often wish they looked as good as their own pictures!

Are most of my own pictures airbrushed? Well I'd have to say no—*all* of them are. This is how it's done, ladies and gentlemen. Everyone has tiny little lines on their faces and, unless you are a hundred years old and deeply wrinkled and someone is taking an 'art picture' of you with the theme of 'old age', the pictures are *always* retouched. Some less, some more. But if we are talking of magazines, yes they all are.

It's funny because even I wasn't aware of *how much* they are all retouched till quite recently, when I shot some fun pictures with my cousin (he is a professional photographer). We did the shoot in Czech, in his basement, and I was pouring water in front of my face so he could get the arty affect of water in motion and parts of my face showing through it. We had tons of fun but later when I saw the images, I was shocked to see that I had so many new lines on my face. 'God, I really have grown old, haven't I?' I thought to myself. It was only later that I realized, when I did another shoot in Mumbai and saw the photographer retouching the pictures right after we shot them, that it's not that I have new lines—they have always been there (maybe not all of them). It's just that even I never got to see most of the shots before they were retouched. Photographers don't give out un-retouched images to anyone! I suppose it's sweet of them, as they don't want to depress their models!

I could talk for hours about what people do before they go on stage or in front of a camera. Drawing lines on the body to create 'muscles' or wearing big boob or buttock pads inside your undergarments are standard. When I was in *Jhalak*, I didn't really do anything more than attach a thousand hairpieces to my hair, making it look long and beautiful (I had really short hair then). Sometimes we had to colour part of my skull black because I am actually bald . . . ha ha ha. No, I'm not, but hey, I could be! You wouldn't know—get it? All these fantastic people in the industry don't look like that in real life. Most of them do various kinds of things to themselves to look the way they do: hair attachments and transplants, Botox, boob jobs, teeth jobs, nose jobs, or who-knows-what-not jobs . . . Does Beyoncé really have such an amazing butt? I doubt it.

When I was in *Jhalak*, making me look good was the responsibility of a team: I had about four people around me at a time, fixing my dress—stitching it onto me so 'nothing' could be seen, fixing things in my hair, applying make-up, applying lotion on my body, tying my shoe laces. And one more person holding my bottle of water. You can't imagine how stressful reality shows can be. You need to be ready all the time.

But my partner did have the make up artist draw some lines on his stomach a few times, to enhance his abs—this is off the record please. I don't want him to throw me up in the air in one of our famous lifts and then walk away, not catching me . . . ha ha ha. Seriously though, in his case, he really didn't need any tricks to make his stomach look good but every little thing helps right?

The power of thoughts

Sometimes it's not so easy to live with our own selves, is it? Now imagine that you could change all this, you could become the most amazing being. As if a fairy showed up and waved her magic wand and transformed you. Well, the fact is, YOU are that fairy and YOU have all the power available to you. You can become the most perfect human being ever. How? By transforming your mind.

This is my mantra and it should be yours too.

You are not your thoughts.
You may not be able to change your body as easily, but you can always change your thoughts about it.

We are the creators of our thoughts, and therefore we can change them too. Thoughts come and go, just like the events in our life. Remember the last time you were faced with a big problem in your life? Remember how intense it was? How stressed you felt? Then a few days passed, maybe a few weeks, and things cooled down. Slowly, slowly everything became fine again. Yet at the time it seemed as if your world had totally collapsed and you felt there was no way out. Now why is that? It's because we identify with our thoughts too much. When the 'shit hits the fan', we immediately create millions of negative thoughts and they block our view. That's why it seems so hard to find a solution. Only once you relax a little and get some space in between those thoughts can you see the path in front of you and the light guiding you out of all the darkness.

Back to the future

A great trick to deal with stress is to imagine yourself a few days later, getting on with life as usual. When I am really under pressure or unhappy, I visualize the future 'me' and it really helps me calm down as it gives me some perspective on the present moment.

So instead of viewing your thoughts as things that define you or that are inseparable from you, it's better to just take them as clouds passing by in the sky—various shapes, some nice, some not so nice. Be the one who observes the thoughts, who witnesses them, as if you were an outsider. Doubt the thoughts that enter your mind, question them, laugh at them. Remember that we are the creators of our own thoughts; therefore, we are in control.

That's why we need to set up a twenty-four-hour CCTV system in the factory that manufactures our thoughts—our mind. It can be quite unpleasant and exhausting to be a victim of every thought and emotion that passes through our minds, right? The CCTV system (our awareness) can be of great help as it cautions us every time a negative thought enters the house (our mind) and we can then act and protect our valuables (happiness and peace of mind) before anything gets stolen.

Watching our thoughts more attentively is just like switching the light on in our minds to get a closer look at what's in there. I'm not saying you are in total darkness now, but perhaps a stronger bulb would be better, no? Bottom line: the more aware you become of your thoughts, the less power they will have over your emotions, and you will gain more control over your life and your ability to relate to the world.

An exercise for those negative thoughts

A good way to start monitoring your negative thoughts is to get a notebook and carry it with you wherever you go and keep writing down all the negative thoughts you get during the day. Or you could email them to yourself or save them on your phone. In the evening sit down with the notebook and go through the list.

Here are some examples:

- Oh God I feel so tired, I wish I didn't have to wake up so early today.
- This day sucks, look at the weather!
- Man the traffic is just mad, I hate this city!
- This is all hopeless . . . I'll never get this right . . . What's the point?
- I feel so unattractive . . .

Now break these thoughts up into small pieces. Ask yourself the following questions. Where does this thought come from? What triggered it? Is it really true? Did I really need to complain about this? Is it that bad? Do I have to look at the worst side of things? Do I just keep complaining about the same thing over and over again but never do anything about it? Is it worth it? Does it change anything?

Once you develop this ability to question, you won't believe every negative thought that enters your mind. You will begin to see it as just something that your mind has created, something that you can be in control of before it makes you develop negative emotions inside you.

Reprogramme the negativity

So how do we reprogramme negative thoughts? There are a number of ways. You can try all of them or only some.

For every negative thought or belief, create a positive one

If you do the writing exercise, you can also spend some time in the evening to read the thoughts, think about them and then see if you can write a positive statement next to each negative thought.

For example, here's what I do:

Negative thought 'Oh God, this city is driving me crazy! This never-ending traffic all the time! And they keep digging the roads but nothing really becomes better anyway!'

Positive thought 'Well, it's the same story every day, so why waste my energy worrying about it? I love this city and that's why I choose to live here. This place has given me so much. It has helped me to learn and evolve as a person, it made me meet so many nice people and experience so many interesting things. So what if I'm stuck in traffic every day; at least I have a car! Some don't even have that.'

Negative thought 'Oh this is just such a bad day. Everything just has to go wrong at the same time! My boss has just screamed at me, I just tore my new scarf that cost me seven bloody thousand and in the evening I have to go to my mother-in-law's and pretend to be this good girl so I please everyone, oh God!'

Positive thought 'Thank God I've got this job to do even though it's a bit shitty at times. So many people are jobless in this city and struggle, but at least I still get my paycheque at the end of the month so I can buy things like this pretty scarf. As for the mother-in-law, how about I bring her flowers tonight?'

Use positive affirmations

Every thought you think and every word you say is an affirmation. Being aware of this, it's apparent one should create positive affirmations instead of negative ones (which we often do unconsciously). Using positive affirmations can help you to feel better about yourself (and your body), change your thinking patterns and also help you to achieve whatever you want to achieve. It is like brainwashing yourself with the good stuff. What is fascinating about affirmations is that the more we use them, the more we behave according to them.

Here's how to make positive affirmations:

1. Always use the present tense: 'I have a beautiful house' instead of 'I will have a beautiful house', or 'I am rich' instead of 'I am going to be rich'. That's because the subconscious mind works with the information it gets *literally* so if you say 'I will be rich', it will all stay in the future.

2. Always use positive sentences (don't use negatives such as the words 'don't' or 'not'). For example: 'I am healthy' instead of 'I am *not* ill', 'I am happy' instead of 'I *don't* feel any worries'. Somehow the mind just doesn't work with the negatives as it ignores the 'not' or 'don't' and focuses on the other words.
3. Focus on feeling the affirmation to be true. If you keep saying I am healthy, but don't *believe* it's possible for you to get healthy, do you think your body will get the message to start healing?
4. Repeat them as often as possible and watch out for thinking negatively the rest of the day, because that would negate the effects of the positive words.

Your affirmations can be about anything you want in your life. Being healthy, safe, secure, happy, rich—anything you want. To give you an example, these are a few of my affirmations:

- I am super healthy, vibrant and energetic.
- I am more and more creative each day and have brilliant new ideas and inspirations coming to me at all times.
- I am very comfortable financially.
- I am happier and happier every day.
- I love myself more and more every day.

I'm sure you get the idea. Don't underestimate affirmations. They are more powerful than you can imagine, just as any thoughts are.

Give yourself a gratitude mantra

Create a little gratitude mantra for yourself. This can be just three sentences (a mini list of things you are grateful for) that you say to yourself every time you feel negative. Focusing your attention on your gratitude mantra will not only get you out of the negative thinking rut but it will remind you that you are truly lucky for the things you already have. I often thank God for having hands when I see someone without them and so on. So when you feel negative just stop doing what you're doing and look around you for a moment and be thankful for what you have, starting with being alive.

My short gratitude mantra goes something like this:

I am grateful for being alive and having this healthy body. I am grateful for having people in my life who love me and who help me and support me whenever I need. I am grateful for all the things that happen in my life, including the bad or challenging ones, as they teach me the most. Thank you.

And here's the extended version:

I am grateful that I have two legs so I can dance, move, walk, run or swim—all of which make me so happy. I am grateful that I have enough money to buy food and don't have to worry about it. I am grateful that I am being loved and cared for and that I have someone to call when I feel low. I am grateful to be able to hear so I can listen to music that makes me so happy. I am grateful that I have hands and fingers so I can write, take care of myself and touch those I love. I am grateful that I have a voice so I can sing, hum along, laugh, cry and say things that matter. I am grateful I have a heart that feels so much, so I can give out my love to the world.

Let's get physical

Often a little shake-up of the body or focusing on breathing can give us that instant hit of positivity and energy. While the mental exercises work in a long-term way, these little tricks are a good way to deal with an overwhelming moment.

Shake it off

Whenever you feel upset, disturbed, angry or just plain tired, there is one easy technique that will get you out of it right away. Find a place where you can be undisturbed for at least five minutes. Then stand with your spine straight in the middle of the room, close your eyes and root yourself by spreading your weight equally between both of your feet. Bend your knees slightly and then start shaking your entire body as if electricity were running through you. Keep your knees loose and move your pelvis up and down. Keep your hands and head relaxed and let them follow the movement and rhythm of the whole body. At times focus on various body parts separately, paying attention to the movement of the particular part and losing control over it, trying to relax it even more. Let your head swing in any direction following the movement of the entire body; let your hands move freely around your body. Don't forget to breathe!

You can shake vigorously or gently. Feel free to shake in whatever way you find comfortable; just pay attention to your feet staying on the ground. The point is that your feet have to feel pinned down while the rest of your body should be totally relaxed, like a tree swaying in the wind but rooted to the earth. Imagine you are shaking off all the negativity inside you and, at the same time, awakening your body and each of your organs.

If you get tired, pause for a bit, take two, three, deep breaths, stretch your arms, rotate your head, loosen up your shoulders and then gently start shaking again. This technique will not just release various tensions inside your body but will also break the negative thinking process. Shaking your head vigorously and making weird sounds is super effective too. My only advice is to find a spot where you're on your own. Because you are going to look very odd to others when you are doing this. You can do some visualization too, which I find works really well. Imagine you are wet and dirty, as if you fell into a muddy pond. Now shake each part of your body, imagining all the mud and water flying off. What fun!

Scream it out

Repressing any negative emotions and not expressing them creates an energy block in the throat chakra. Chakra is a Sanskrit word that means wheel, spinning ball or a centre. Chakras are the body's energy centres, they are the openings for the life energy to flow in and out of our aura, the energy field that surrounds the physical body. The throat chakra is the seat of self expression and by keeping 'in' things we need to say to others but don't, or by not acting out what we feel, we are obstructing (and compromising) the energy flow in our bodies.

It's important not to stop yourself from making sounds of pain or pleasure when you feel those emotions. It's the most natural thing, yet we are often afraid to do it. Being vocal when making love is one of those situations, for example. Most people are afraid of making any sounds while lovemaking, which is really sad because that's what makes it all much more exciting, but mainly because it's unnatural to hold those sounds in and it obstructs the energy flow during sex. I'd suggest you be as vocal as you can!

Of course when the sound you need to express is of pain or anger, it might be quite scary if someone else is witnessing it. That's where my little fun 'technique' comes in. Screaming into a pillow is quite an obvious choice, but why wait to get home and get hold of a pillow? I do this in my car as I drive. Yes, in the middle of Mumbai's traffic, I drive my Honda Accord, screaming my lungs out like a psycho. Sometimes I yell at a high pitch till I run out of breath, then breathe in and start again. Sometimes I use bad words (Czech abuses generally, though I sometimes use the Hindi ones too). It's a lot of fun. Try it some time. You'll have fun, you'll get the bad stuff out of your system for sure and you'll feel more alive and free at the end of it. (And no, don't worry. No one outside the car can hear a thing. And if they do, SO WHAT?)

Beat it out

This technique is lots of fun. What you need to do is to close yourself in a room (lock the door if possible), fetch a big pillow or cushion and then beat the shit out of it. Simple, but oh so effective! You should go on and on and have no mercy with the pillow till you get all the negativity, anger and pissed-off-ness out of your system. Think of the pillow as your enemy and the very thing (or person) that is responsible for all your troubles, all your stress, worries and in fact EVERY SINGLE THING that EVER went wrong in your life! Yes! Have no mercy and get your revenge! Scream (into the pillow) too, cry, shout your lungs out, do whatever helps you to get the emotions out and makes you feel free. At the end of this super release technique you should be lying exhausted on the bed but feeling you can finally breathe freely and laugh at yourself for being mad.

My only advice is, don't use any of those pretty-looking (or expensive) cushions—take the ugliest pillow or cushion you have and kill it! Murder it! You'll be glad you did. It's really not healthy to keep the negativity inside you.

Breathe it out

Sit or lie down in a relaxed position. Then take a deep breath and as you breathe in imagine a white light entering through the top of your head (this is where the crown chakra is). Let the light spread all over your body as you breathe in. It's almost as if you were sucking the light in through your head. Then as you breathe out, imagine you are exhaling through your stomach (this is where most of the tension is locked in) and what is coming out is dark grey or black smoke. Keep repeating this cycle for as long as you wish or till you start feeling relief. Keep breathing in the light and breathing out the smoke. If you feel any physical pain in other parts of your body (the heart or throat for example, as your energy may be stuck at that point as well), imagine the black smoke coming out of there. At the end of this, once you feel the tension is gone, focus on visualizing the light getting brighter and stronger, bathing your body in rainbow colours and when you exhale imagine the darkness diminishing slowly with each exhalation, getting lighter and lighter as your body is now free of the negativity.

Fat thoughts

For years, much of my negativity was tied to the way I felt about my body. I called those negative thoughts my fat thoughts. If you have some extra weight, it's likely you are very familiar with fat thoughts too, although you may not call them that. Even if you are very confident otherwise, and very successful or talented, you will still feel imperfect if you're not in shape. The horrible fat thoughts will come and torture you, especially at key moments—when you go on a date, apply for a new job or enter any new environment. They are always there. You judge yourself and you are afraid that you will be judged.

Fat thoughts make us look fat

Have you ever wondered why some people don't really look fat or 'seem' fat even though they are in fact overweight? You may have a friend whom you wouldn't think of calling 'fat', but when you think of it, she or he actually has some extra kilos on, while there are others on whom you notice even just a little bit of extra weight they may have put on. Isn't that peculiar? And you know why that is? I believe that those who don't perceive themselves as overweight or have no bad feelings about it give out a very different vibe. And so even the world around them doesn't perceive them as overweight! (Unless they are of course very, very big). It's interesting isn't it? That's another example of your inner world (and the state of your mind) reflecting onto the external world. For example, I have this friend who really doesn't worry about her weight that much (she certainly doesn't think it is what does or doesn't make her beautiful) and as a result I too would never describe her as a 'fat' person. She is just the way she is and there is no need for her to 'fix' anything about herself. While another friend of mine, who has just a tiny amount of fat on her belly is so conscious of it that whenever I see her I think that maybe it would be good if I shared some weight-loss tips with her. Now I don't think she needs to fix anything—she really is NOT fat—but because she thinks she is, I also get this message from her.

I often watch other people around me when I travel and see who is relaxed in their body and who is not. It's encrypted deeply in their body language and I suppose I can recognize it easily because I know how I myself used to be conscious of my body and always used to adjust the way I sat, stood or walked. We can be so conscious about the way we move, stand or sit. I have a friend who even sucks her cheeks in whenever a photo is being taken just to look slimmer. (I've got some really funny images of her trying to pull this off.)

For those of us who have eating-disorder-type of behaviour, fat thoughts are always there somewhere, especially when the mind is free. You end up waiting for the day when you finally lose the weight and get free of these fat thoughts. But the day never comes my friend. You won't be free of these thoughts by losing the kilos. The fear of gaining it all back will always be there, and as long as that fear is alive, so are the fat thoughts.

Confronting those fat thoughts

Now tell me, how do you feel around the word 'fat'? Is the 'fat' taking up a lot of space in your head? Technically it is because, if you remember, more than sixty percent of the dry weight of the brain is actually made up of fat. But that's not what I am talking about right now. Tell me, if you were walking through a hotel lobby and overheard someone who you just passed by say the word 'fat' would you worry it could have related to you?

Close your eyes for a minute and say the word FAT a few times and watch what thoughts it brings. What feelings does it evoke? Talking about it helps the most in tackling the discomfort connected to the issue. Imagine sitting down with your boyfriend or a partner and telling him, 'Look I have an issue with my weight. I am not comfortable with my body; I feel imperfect. I feel conscious whenever I eat a piece of chocolate. I feel conscious wearing tight clothes. I feel conscious being naked in front of you.'

Can you do this? Can you talk about it openly? It's difficult, right? But it helps. It really, really does. Admitting it to the world helps you to accept it too. I really feel so free now after I have admitted to having an eating disorder. Every time someone asks me what the book I am writing is about, I say: 'Well, I have had an eating disorder for over seventeen years and the book is about (. . . and then I go on for hours)'. I say this to total strangers and I don't mind at all. Amazing, isn't it? It was something I was ashamed of for so long, and now I can tell anyone.

My advice to all men

Here's a little bit of invaluable advice for all the men reading this book. This counsel will save you guys from countless potential fights with the women in your life. The advice is: DO NOT EVER combine the two words 'you' and 'fat' in one sentence about any woman you like, particularly if you want her to like you back.

When your woman asks you, 'Baby, do you think I've put on weight?', your reply should be, 'What are you saying? No way! In fact, I think you might have lost some!' This is the only safe answer, okay? Got it? This is for your own good, I swear! Oh, and one more thing. You need to provide the answer

IMMEDIATELY! Because if you pause and think and only then blurt this out, the woman will see that and you're not going to get away with it. Watch out you guys, this is a very sensitive topic for most women.

Have you ever come across any woman who has openly told you she was raped? I have. And I could see the power in this woman's eyes. She was able to say it because she had dealt with it—saying it out loud was one of her ways of doing so.

So let's deal with the fat and throw some light on it, shall we? Write down the answer to these few questions.

- What feelings come up when you think of the word 'fat'?
- What do you feel if you imagine someone calling you fat?
- Do you feel anger? Self-pity? Do you feel unlucky or that the world is unfair because you cannot be as thin as others and you put on weight so easily?
- Do you always gain weight when you are facing difficult situations?
- Can you find a way to accept the fat?
- What is fat to you? What kind of feelings do you associate it with?
- Imagine yourself thin for a while. How do you feel? Do you feel like a different person? Do you feel more fragile? Does the fat give you a feeling of security? Could you be using it as 'protection' against the world outside?
- Are you sure you really are overweight? Who do you compare yourself with? Is it because you have

thin friends that you feel uncomfortable, or do you feel discriminated against at work because of the way you look?

- If you were living completely alone on an island, would you mind the fat?
- Do you call yourself fat? Can you avoid using harsh words when describing yourself? Are you sure you are not trying to fit into some norms that perhaps aren't even healthy or natural for your body and the way it's built?
- Who sets these norms anyway?

These are just cues to spark some thoughts. Now take a sheet of paper and write a confession to yourself, write down all the unhappy feelings you have about your body, what it makes you feel, how it makes you conscious, how it makes you uncomfortable. Do you feel angry about it? What do you feel? Write it down.

Now go to the person who is the closest to you (say, your best friend or your partner) and read your confession out to them. Then talk about it as openly as you can. You will see, this will empower you. And it's quite likely that the person you share this with will also have similar feelings and experiences to deal with. We all do. That brings a lot of relief and helps you to come closer to self-acceptance too.

If you feel coming out of the closet and sharing this with someone was beneficial, try to do it several times or as many times as it takes to make you feel comfortable talking about it. If you are a woman, I'd even suggest calling a few of your friends home one night and having an open discussion. Men have a very different way of relating and I can't imagine they would discuss such a thing in a circle with other men. So, to my male readers, I'd suggest you talk to your girlfriends or a female friend instead. But please do it.

If you are a woman, though, take advantage of the fact that women can open up like this with other women and use the support of your closest friends. Call them home, have tea and cake (Yes! Cake! That might bring extra inspiration) and talk, share . . . rip apart the topic of fat and your feelings about your body. You will have fun too! The more you talk about it, the more healing it is and the more you will be able to relax about carrying a little extra weight. Hearing that others feel as bad will also give you support. You are not alone.

How to get free from fat thoughts

This is where the earlier section on negativity comes in. You deal with fat thoughts the way you deal with all negative thoughts. The same principles are at play.

Become aware of your thought patterns

Negativity is a habit, a habit you can train yourself to 'unlearn'. So the first step is to become aware of the fat thoughts as you should be aware of any negative thoughts.

Replace fat thoughts with loving ones

Fat thought 'Oh God, I look so fat in this dress! And my butt looks giant!'

Positive thought 'This colour looks really nice on me. I remember I got many compliments on this dress the last time. So what if my butt is big, at least I have one! Plus my sense of humour beats it all, so why should I worry about my behind so much?'

Do this with whatever fat thoughts you have. It's hard to get rid of them completely and they will keep coming long after you have relaxed about your body shape. Remember this is how your mind has been used to functioning, so these thoughts will not disappear right away. Even now I struggle with my fat thoughts.

Shift your focus

Think of all your role models—the people who have contributed to your life, the community or the world. Was their appearance essential or important to their achievements?

You get fat thoughts only when you give your looks too much importance. Shift your focus from the outside to the inside. You are so much more than what others perceive you to be! You have so much to offer, and you know it! And you know that there are things inside you that make you a good human being. So remind yourself of this once in a while. In fact, why don't you make a list of all the things that are special about you and put it under a pillow and read it before you sleep? Or hang it somewhere or hide it in a special place if you don't want others to see it. It's good to remind yourself of your inner qualities at times when you feel powerless for whatever reason. Many self-empowerment books suggest their readers make a list like this. I have done it several times myself and always enjoyed it. It will make you feel really positive, so come on, fetch a pen and paper and start. And don't you try to be brief!

Deal with the thin fantasy

Tell me, what do you think you will get from losing weight? Happiness? More acceptance from the outside world? More respect or admiration? A better job? A better boyfriend or girlfriend, or a great husband or wife? Is losing weight the best way to go about getting those things? What makes you think that the 'thin' you get this more easily than the 'fat' you? Don't you think this is a fantasy? A dream?

Try another exercise. Write down all that you believe you can do if only you were thinner. Now think about those statements for a while. Can't you really do all those things being your old self, instead of being this new thin person you want to become? What is stopping you really? The fat?

Here are some examples:

- When I'm thin, I'll have many friends and everyone will love me.
- When I'm thin, I won't be so shy about talking to men (or women) and will finally find a good relationship.
- When I'm thin, I'll go on a trip to Thailand and feel comfortable on the beach in a bikini (or swimming trunks).
- When I'm thin, I will meet the man (or woman) of my dreams and marry him (or her).
- When I'm thin, I will not be depressed anymore.
- When I'm thin, everyone will admire me.
- When I'm thin, I'll travel the world.

Learning to love yourself

Hopefully these exercises will make you more aware of the negativity and anxieties you feel about your body, and help you combat them. But I think it's worth doing some exercises that are more physical and help you to actually enjoy your body. And once you can do that, you are on the path to love and acceptance. You might find that some of these exercises make you uncomfortable—those are the ones you should do, because those are the areas you need to work on.

Facing the mirror

Do you often avoid looking at yourself in the mirror, especially when you're naked? Sometimes this is a good thing, as the less you check yourself, the less you bash yourself. If you're someone like me—too conscious of or almost obsessed with your physical imperfections—you know what a relief it can be when you don't get to see your body in the mirror for a few days. I was always relieved when I would go on vacation and stay in a place with just a small mirror in the bathroom. I am sure some of you will relate to that feeling!

However, avoiding the mirror because you're uncomfortable with your body and don't want to face the reality or your negative thoughts is not good either. You need to face those thoughts of yours and work on them and not ignore them. So if you've been avoiding the mirror when you're naked start doing the opposite. Make sure you take time to look at yourself every day before or after you take a shower. And if you don't have the courage to do this every day, start with once a week and move up.

I know it can be scary if you've never done this! Look at yourself from all angles in the mirror and don't pay attention to any negative thoughts that enter your mind. Instead think or say aloud to yourself: 'I love each and every inch of my body. I am perfect the way I am. I am beautiful and I deserve all the love—all the love I get, all the love I can have and all the love in the world.' With these words, touch whatever areas you are uncomfortable with and feel acceptance and love towards them as you caress them with your hands. At the same time say to each of those parts, 'You don't need to change in any way. I love you the way you are.' Then smile at yourself in the mirror. Feel the care for your body as you would feel for your lover. I even kiss my own shoulders at times, which makes me feel cute and smile right away! Does this sound too corny? Well, it might be, but I promise you it's worth it. You can use your own words and your own gestures, but the point of the exercise is to make love to yourself in a way.

Loving touch

I sometimes use the opportunity to give my body extra love as I apply cream or oil on my body after a shower. I massage the cream into every part of my skin, doing it very slowly, often closing my eyes too. During this time I savour the way my skin feels, the way it smells, its cleanliness. I think of how the cream or oil is hydrating me, making my body feel smoother. I have a friend who bathes with the lights switched off and a candle on for the same reason. It's all about creating delicious rituals for yourself where you like being with your body and enjoy it. I know it's hard to find the time or the head space. I myself don't do this most days but I do love it when I do. If you can, get massages as often as it's possible. It's really part of the same thing.

Belly Love

If there is something you find hard to accept about your midsection (your belly), as I do, focus on relaxing it as many times a day as you can (as you sit in a meeting, work at your desk or walk around somewhere). We are often used to having our belly muscles tense and not breathing deeply, which compromises the energy flow in our body.

In the Chinese, Korean and Japanese traditions, the centre of the belly is the place where one's strength and wisdom is hidden as that's where the *hara* point is located (three finger-widths below and two finger-widths behind the navel). In Japanese the word hara means stomach, abdomen or belly; the Chinese call this point the low *dantian*, which can be loosely translated as 'elixir field'—the Taoists translate it as the 'sea of energy'.

The hara is considered the physical centre of balance and gravity of the human body and the centre of one's internal energy (chi). This is where we once received energy (through the umbilical cord) from our mother and it is where we connect to the universal life force. Even in yoga the hara is thought to be the seat of prana (meaning the vital force in Sanskrit) that radiates outwards to the entire body and it is considered to be an important point of focus when practicing meditation techniques.

Many people have energy blockages in this area. Being disconnected or having an energy blockage in the hara is believed to be a cause of many addictions especially to food, and over-eating is a sign of a blocked hara. Focusing on the hara point and breathing into it will make you feel more grounded, helping foster the ability to deal better with issues and to maintain good health and recover from illnesses.

Take deep breaths into the belly as many times during the day as possible, relaxing into it as much as you can and try to locate the hara. As you do this regularly, you will begin to feel more centred and in the present moment. I often place my hand on my belly and walk around like that, noticing how the belly expands as I take each breath, making it as relaxed as possible. Sometimes I even caress my belly as if I had a baby in there, giving it my love just as I would to a baby.

Partner exercises

Having your partner assure you that he/she loves you as you are, even the parts of your body that you dislike, can be very healing and helpful along the way to accepting your body. Stand in front of each other naked or in lingerie and tell each other what you like about each other. Then share the parts of your body you dislike or are uncomfortable with and ask your partner to help you love those areas, accept them and relax about them. Your partner can then touch and caress those areas and tell you how she/he likes them the way they are, and you do the same to him/her in return. You can also tell each other what is sexy about the other's body and what you like the most. Plan to do this on a relaxed evening when you know you won't be disturbed. It's enough if you do this just once, as long as you don't forget to keep giving your love and attention to your partner's body and those areas she/he is insecure about.

Teach your partner how to make love to you

Do you find it difficult to tell your partner what you like him to do for you in bed? You probably do, even if you are quite a free-spirited and open-minded person. It's just not the kind of conversation that comes up between telling your boyfriend what you ate for lunch and deciding what movie you should go to watch tonight. It's one of those talks that you plan—first figure out what you're going to say, then choose the best time and the best situation and then you start.

'Babyyyyy?????' . . . [pause]

'What, baby?' says your baby.

'Well, you know' . . . [another pause]

'What, baby?' Now he knows something is brewing.

You flutter your eyelashes, blush and then start stammering and stumbling over your words.

'What is it?!!' he says, getting impatient and a little irritated.

That slight irritation in his voice scares you away and you quickly say, 'Oh nothing, forget it.'

You feel sad now and a little upset at him for getting irritated so quickly. And before you know it, the moment is gone and you don't feel like talking about the subject. Sounds familiar?

First of all, however great your partner is and however much he loves you, he is not telepathic—he needs to be taught about your body. We are all different; so even if he's been with several women before you, it's always like starting from scratch. You need to stop waiting for the day that he 'gets it' and just plainly tell him. Tell him 'in words' and not with your intense stares, okay? Don't be scared. He needs to learn how to make love to you simply because you deserve to be made love to in the most beautiful way.

So let me tell you how I do this. I wait for the right moment, such as when we're hanging out in bed. Be careful you don't tell him right after lovemaking—he'll probably think that you are telling him *now* because what you guys just did was unsatisfying! You don't want to do that! Most guys have big egos and even slightly insinuating that he is not the best lover you have ever had is very, very dangerous! So you want to wait for the right time, when you're just cuddling and chilling for example, and then say:

'Babyyyy? I would like to learn how to make love to you. Can you tell me the things you like?'

What he is going to say is: 'Well I like everything you do!'

This answer sucks as it doesn't get you anywhere. So you say, 'Well, I'm glad you do, but you know, I want to be even better than that, cause I love you and I want to make you happy.'

'But you are great!' he will insist.

What you need to do is to give him specific examples. See, he is not going to get creative here and surprise you by talking openly about the subject—he is as shy as you are right now. So you need to help him out. Give him concrete examples; give him choices. Ask him if he likes it better this way or that way, the option A or option B technique. Then all he has to do is to say yes or no. Now after you have figured out what he likes and how he likes it, he will obviously think of turning the same question towards you and ask you how YOU like it, right?

Well, no. He won't. And if he does, PLEASE! Marry him NOW!!!!

Most men will just not think to ask you the same thing back. I really don't know why. It's a mystery to me. So what you need to do is to simply prompt him:

'Baby?'

'Yes?'

'Would you also like to know what I like?'

'Of course I would!' he says quickly, FIIINALY realizing he should have asked you this a few years ago!

And that's when you will tell him all. If you find it difficult to talk about certain things (and you probably will), just be honest and tell him how shy you feel talking about it and it would help you if he was also prompting you with questions. He gladly will (he has no option now anyway).

See? Is it that difficult? Now don't delay having this conversation, okay? There are plenty of things you need to share and it is essential to making your relationship stronger and better. Take it as an order given by me, one of the things you *have* to do.

P.S.: I know you must be wondering why I am giving you sex tips but I do think your sexual relationship with your partner really affects the way you feel about yourself. Plus, I couldn't resist!

Connect with your body

This simple technique is a great way to start your day while you're still lying in bed, or you can do it any time during the day and as often as you wish—the more often, the better.

There are no particular steps as it's all about following what your body needs in that moment, but the basic idea is that you become a cat for a few minutes and stretch your entire body as if this were the last stretch you'll ever do in your life. Now I am not saying stretch just *like* the cat does it. I said 'become' the cat. The idea is that you should go fully into it and forget you have this human body that is used to moving in any particular way. You are not supposed to 'think' here and then do the stretch just like you are used to doing in the gym. Forget all that.

Close your eyes first, take a long deep breath and then, as you are about to exhale, spread your hands and legs into space in any direction that feels good. You can do this lying down, sitting or standing, or start from a sitting position (if you are working at a desk, let's say, although your colleagues might giggle at you!) and then stand up or slide down from the chair onto the floor (this can be done as one of the 'stretches'). The idea is to keep breathing and 'expanding' and making various, and even weird-looking, moves and positions as long as it feels pleasant and relieves any tension or stiffness in your body. Move your entire body from your head to your fingers and toes at the same time.

If you lie down on the floor to do this, make sure the floor is comfortable and not unpleasantly cold. You can do this on a bed or an exercise mat, if you wish. I prefer not to use the yoga mat as, when I'm lying on the floor, I tend to slide on it. Rotate your head from side to side, up and down, rotate your whole body, your core (torso), your feet, etc. Just become the cat and move in whatever way feels good, create weird positions, scrunch up your face so you stretch your facial muscles too and be as vocal as you can. The purpose of this exercise is not just to stretch for health benefits but to reconnect with your body and learn to like being in it a bit more.

And now for some instant tips

Here are some quick and out-of-the box fixes for feeling happier in your skin. Don't believe that these can help? Try them!

Wear comfy clothes

I would strongly suggest you stop wearing clothes that make you feel conscious of your body shape in any way. Tight clothes often do that to us. Even if you have a great figure, I think it's important to stop focusing on the body image that you project. You are not your body!

I used to be so conscious of the fact that I was 'supposed' to look hot, because I was a model, that I would always end up wearing some tight, 'model-like' clothes. I have to say I never felt really relaxed in those clothes. When I 'grew up' (mentally) and realized I didn't really need any male attention to feel confident or good about myself anymore, I started wearing loose-fitting clothes. I also didn't care to project that I was a model—I knew I was good at my job and therefore didn't need to prove anything. Let me tell you, it feels great when you don't need to impress anyone!

Cook for yourself

You may not be a good cook, or not even particularly into it. I never used to cook either unless I was with a boyfriend or my husband. I felt I could do more creative things with my time—food once it's eaten is gone, while spending that time writing a song seemed more productive. Then, just a few months ago, I started feeling the urge to cook, even though there was no one in my life. Eating someone else's food, even if it is prepared by my maid (and she is a fantastic cook) or eating at a five-star restaurant just doesn't do it anymore. So I figured it was not about the food being nutritious. What I longed for was to look after myself, give my body some special love. Love makes us do things we would never do otherwise, isn't it? Self-love is no different.

Get rid of the weighing scale

Should some numbers or some statistics tell you if you are in shape or not? You ARE in shape—YOUR shape! Now focus on loving that shape first of all. Sure you should work towards improving it, but that doesn't mean you should dislike the current 'you'. Weighing yourself often can affect you negatively. Forget the numbers.

Pamper your body, pamper your soul

You know best what 'pampering' means to you. Massage sounds like the obvious option but, as strange as it is for me to understand, there are people on this earth who don't like massages. The only way I can explain this is that they have never experienced a good one. The best massage I have ever received was not from a trained masseur in an exotic five-star Thailand spa but by Farrokh Chhotia in his studio in Mumbai when I shot my first Lakmé campaign. Anyway, pampering yourself is a must. Massages, hot baths and beauty-parlour visits should be on your schedule. Why? Because you love you and because you deserve it! That's why. Pampering your body pampers your soul at the same time. When I'm going through heartache, I always start pampering myself right away (my body AND my soul). I'll go for a pedicure to my favourite pedicure hero, whose 'hello' makes me feel loved instantly, or I will go to the Taj Land's End's coffee shop and treat myself to a glass of wine and listen to the piano playing and hum along. Now these are my tricks. I am sure you have yours—so start now.

Finally

In this section I have moved away from our bodies and spread my net a bit wider. But as I have said all through this book, ultimately you have to love yourself before you love your body. So what does loving yourself mean? To me it's simple—it's never criticizing yourself and unconditionally accepting who you are. Is this easy to do? No, it isn't really. But it's not that hard either. It just needs some awareness, focus and practice—three things which I hope I have helped you with in this section. But the most important thing you need is time. You and I both know that it's going to take some time for us to be able to stop criticizing ourselves. This is what we've been doing all our lives! How many negative inner dialogues do have we during just one day? How many times do we tell ourselves: 'Oh God, I'm so stupid! I'm an idiot! Damn! I hate myself and I hate hating myself!'

There is no need to feel that you're under any pressure just because you keep getting upset with yourself for whatever reason or are having a critical inner dialogue. Thinking to yourself: 'Oh God, I am being negative again, damn!' doesn't really help. Don't beat yourself up for not loving yourself enough! That would be counterproductive. It's going to take some time for sure, but that's all right.

The thing about love, too, is that it is so individual. Unlike Part 2, where eating a certain way will almost certainly have an effect on your body, the tips and techniques I have given you in this section may not all work for you. I bet you even turned up your nose at some of them! But some will speak to you and you may have smiled to yourself already while reading them. That's how you know it may be a good one for you to implement. So go for it. The more crazy or unusual those ideas are, the better it is, as it's quite likely they will also make you feel more alive and free.

When you start feeling positive and loving towards yourself, the world around you will change as well. My motto in life is: 'Don't change the world, change yourself!' And that's pretty much what Gandhi used to say after all: 'Be the change you wish to see.' Now, loving yourself, you will simply create more love in this world, and then the world will start changing on its own. You'll see . . .

Goodbye

It's time for a goodbye. I have to say this is an emotional moment for me. Writing this book has taught me so much about me. It's been an incredible journey (and not always an easy one). It all started after one simple phone call I received one morning from a friend of mine about five years ago, 'Yaana, can you give me some fitness tips? I'm really desperate to lose some weight and nothing I've tried so far seems to have worked. I'm just really fed up now; can you help me out please?' Two hours later we were still talking on the phone (no actually WE were not talking, I was). Fitness has always been my passion, and she was eager to listen to all I had to say.

When we finally hung up, I looked at the time and realized that I had just broken my record of non-stop talking and I had to laugh. 'Hell, I should do this for a living!' I thought. Of course it's not that I wanted to earn some extra bucks with it. What I wanted was to feel as inspired and alive as I did while having that phone conversation. It really gave me a lot of energy, as I could feel I was helping someone and I knew how. I realized then how inspiring it was for me to share what I have learnt and truly believe in, knowing that it could help someone to change their life for the better, improve their health and perhaps even direct them towards a happier life in some way. How wonderful would it be to be able to do that often, I thought. What else could make me more satisfied in my life?

But as I started writing the book, I began to realize that this could not be an ordinary fitness book. I began to look at my own life, all the fears and insecurities I had suffered from, which led me to be obsessed with fitness and dieting in the first place. I began to ask myself and my friends, why was it that we were so obsessed by weight loss? Why were most of us never happy with the way we were? I realized that it all comes down to how much we really love ourselves and that no fitness tip would really work if you didn't resolve some of the stuff in your head. And so I decided to write a book that would ultimately be about loving ourselves. It would combine all my years of learning about fitness and health but it would also use my own experiences in finally coming to a place where I liked myself. I decided to tell you all the mistakes I made, all the nightmares I suffered from, all the crazy things I did, alongside the lessons I ultimately learnt. I wanted not just to be your teacher in this book but a fellow traveller. In fact as I say through the book, I am still on this journey. I still sometimes see food as being 'good' or 'bad', I still look at myself in pictures and go, 'Oh God I look a bit overweight in this.' I still feel tempted to go on a no-carb diet once in a while (though I quickly stop myself!).

Loving yourself is sooo much harder than losing weight, let me tell you! It's a lifetime of work. But every day I get stronger and I hope this book does the same for you too. So thank you my dear friend for listening to me for all this while.

If you feel what you have read has made you stop and think, change some of the ways you behave and begin to look at why you do what you do, then pass on the message. Each of us has the power to change the world around us in some way and I believe that all we need is LOVE.

Acknowledgements

First of all I would like to thank my teacher Cuckoo whom I simply cannot ever thank enough for teaching me not just about healing, the body and acupuncture, but also about life. Thank you Cuckoo for giving me your love and support all this time.

I'd also like to thank my editors Chiki Sarkar and Ameya Nagarajan who helped me to transform this book into what it is and everyone else at Penguin who has worked on the project. Thank you my dear Penguins for making this happen.

Special thanks from the bottom of my heart also goes to my dear friend Ankur Tewari who was the one who encouraged me to start writing this book and who always believed in me, even when I didn't.

And at the end I would like to thank myself. Like seriously, I deserve some huge credit for this because I have gone crazy trying to write this book over the years. I rewrote it four times, I struggled with learning how to even write to begin with as I had no experience with it whatsoever. So I'd like to thank myself for not giving up whenever I felt frustrated, exhausted, stuck and fed up with it all. After all I did also get rewarded by feeling inspired, excited, thrilled and happy as I believed what I was writing could help many others who have struggled with similar issues I did.

At the end, I'd like to thank the Universe (the existence, God or whatever you call it) for giving me brains so I could think, fingers so I could type, heart so I could feel and all the troubles so I could learn.

Appendix

These are few links to shops I have been using to order high quality supplements or other health foods.

USA
http://www.sunfood.com/
http://www.sunwarrior.com/
(This company manufactures the vegan protein powder I mentioned. There are suppliers in the United Kingdom and some places in Asia too, check which will work out the cheapest for you.)

UK
http://www.fresh-network.com/
http://www.rawliving.eu/

INDIA
www.satvika.in/
(They are an organic food delivery service in Mumbai)